disconnect

bridging the
youth pastor and **senior** pastor
gap

by
Doug Franklin

Every time you walk out of your senior pastor's office, you leave with a sense of bewilderment and confusion. "Did I just waste the last hour? Did he really hear what's going on with our students? Is youth ministry really a priority for this guy?"

Unfortunately, you aren't alone. When it works, the relationship between a youth pastor and senior pastor opens the door to dynamic ministry in the local church. But when that relationship is weak, damaged, or broken, it can create an environment that breeds frustration, dissension, and burnout.

And in far too many churches, that relationship *is* weak, damaged, or broken. Trust, respect, and sacrifice don't happen when we aren't on the same page. Doug writes directly to you as a youth pastor, offering his encouragement and wisdom.

Doug Franklin and the team at LeaderTreks tackle the challenge of restoring that relationship in *The Disconnect*, a unique resource that brings together youth pastors and senior pastors for honest dialogue on the tough task of working together.

In this book, you'll discover:
- How to more effectively communicate with your senior pastor
- How core values can lead to greater respect
- Why ministry and money can't be separated
- How to align your expectations
- Why a shared mission is essential

If you're on the verge of a breakdown or ready to quit because you just can't take it anymore, you'll want to read this book. Your working relationship might still be restorable. And if it isn't, you can absorb and apply these truths in future ministry settings.

If you and your senior pastor already communicate and work together well, this book will help you solidify that relationship. You can take something good and make it great.

Doug Franklin is the president of LeaderTreks, an innovative leadership development organization focusing on students and youth workers. He and his wife, Angie, live in West Chicago. Doug grew up in Illinois and is a graduate of Wheaton College. His passion is using experiential learning to help students and adults grow as leaders. Doug writes about leadership on his blog at dougfranklinonline.com.

The Disconnect
Bridging the Youth Pastor and Senior Pastor Gap

Copyright © 2011 Doug Franklin

group.com
simplyyouthministry.com

Credits
Author: Doug Franklin
Executive Developer: Nadim Najm
Chief Creative Officer: Joani Schultz
Editor: Michael Novelli
Copy Editors: Rob Cunningham and Janis Sampson
Cover Art and Production: Jeff A. Storm and Veronica Lucas
Production Manager: DeAnne Lear

Unless otherwise indicated, all Scripture quotations are taken from the *Holy Bible*, New Living Translation, copyright © 1996, 2004, 2007. Used by permission of Tyndale House Publishers, Inc., Carol Stream, Illinois 60188. All rights reserved.

Library of Congress Cataloging-in-Publication Data
Franklin, Doug, 1963-
  The disconnect : bridging the youth pastor and senior pastor gap / Doug Franklin.
    p. cm.
  ISBN 978-0-7644-6658-8 (pbk. : alk. paper)
  1. Church youth workers--Professional relationships. 2. Clergy--Professional relationships. I. Title.
  BV4447.F665 2011
  253'.2--dc22
                              2010052915

ISBN 978-0-7644-6658-8

10 9 8 7 6 5 4 3 2 1   20 19 18 17 16 15 14 13 12 11

Printed in the United States of America.

Dedication

This book is dedicated to my beautiful and creative wife,
Angie, who helped with this book more than you'll ever know.
Thank you, sweetheart.

—Doug

Contents

Start Here...

It was my first youth ministry job where I was the lead youth worker. The church was only a couple of years old and didn't yet have a senior pastor, but my youth ministry was thriving. Countless kids, churched and un-churched, were deepening or starting their relationship with Christ. I loved my job, but I knew I needed wisdom and mentoring. Needless to say, I was thrilled when the elders told me they were hiring a senior pastor. Even more exciting was that the new senior pastor was a former youth pastor and a well-known youth speaker. I envisioned a partnership in which he would not only lead me but also mentor me in ministry and in life. Together we would form the foundation of an amazing team, bringing people from all over our city through the doors of our church and into a relationship with Jesus. Our mission would move forward because we would be united.

When the senior pastor arrived, I was already busy planning a mission trip for my group. Having gotten approval from two dads who had been overseeing me, I presented my plan to the senior pastor, and to my delight he told me to "go for it." I continued my planning and even bought a flight ticket (with my senior pastor's approval) to set up the mission site.

Two weeks later I was asked to breakfast by a few elder members and the senior pastor. They didn't waste much time before they were drilling me about the mission trip and chastising me for making all the decisions without any authority. I tried to defend myself, telling them the senior pastor had told me to "go for it," but he claimed he had heard nothing about it. I was shocked and hurt, and for the first time realized the hard truth: My senior pastor and I were disconnected. Six months later I had resigned.

Looking back, I see many of the real problems that were hidden from me then: My senior pastor and I had not spent any real time getting to know each other on a personal or ministry level, we didn't understand each other's values, and we certainly were not on the same mission. Many of these things led to my resignation.

This disconnect saddens me, yet it is all too common. Many youth pastors end up leaving ministry because of unmet expectations regarding the relationship with their senior pastors. Is this the senior pastors' fault? Of course not, but they do need help in realizing the important role they play in keeping their youth pastors in ministry. Things don't go well in a youth ministry when the senior pastor and youth pastor are at odds, not talking, or holding judgments and grudges. The youth ministry, and the church as a whole, doesn't function at its best when the pastoral team is not unified. Trust, respect, and sacrifice don't happen when we aren't on the same page. The need is out there for senior pastors and youth pastors to be unified as they pursue a mission.

 Our churches *can* function with a staff that's not unified. But they *cannot* reach the potential God has dreamed for them.

As I sat down to write this book, I'll admit my time as a youth pastor steered much of my thinking about the subject matter. After all, it is my experiences, good and bad, which have shaped how I've served other youth workers for many years. While my experiences have proved effective in the advice I gave to most youth workers, I realized it could not be the only source material I worked from to write this book. To that end, much of what you read has come from not only my time as a youth worker but also from others around me. Through interviews with youth pastors and senior pastors and through multiple surveys, I gathered the needed information to write this book. Many of their stories are retold in my own words throughout these pages.

A couple of things to know before you start...

1. The comments in boxed text throughout the book mean something. I sent out the finished chapters to youth pastors and senior pastors all around the country to get their specific thoughts regarding the content of this book. As you read, you'll notice this icon 🎤 along with comments or even personal stories relating to the material from many senior pastors who were once youth pastors. Much of the boxed text lends validity to my points, while others offer some pushback. I chose to include all these comments because the pages should display my heart behind this book. There are many opinions out there which deserve to be heard. No single piece of writing or individual conversation will solve all the problems you have in ministry. My hope and prayer is for you to find nuggets of truth contained in my writing or in the boxed text and apply them. If this book brings fruit to the relationship between you and your senior pastor, I have achieved my goal.

2. It takes two to tango. For every chapter written to youth pastors, there's a chapter on the same topic written to senior pastors. I tried to help youth pastors take steps to understand their senior pastors' point of view and I did the same thing for senior pastors. Ideally, you will benefit the most from this book if both you and the senior pastor read it at the same time. Each exercise at the end of the chapter will be more helpful if you can debrief it together, but still beneficial if that's not possible.

3. You don't have to be at your wits' end to read this. I wrote this book because so many youth pastors came to me exasperated and ready to quit. If your relationship with your senior pastor is good, there is a lot of stuff in here that can help move it from good to great—from tweaking your communication style to gaining a common language and understanding of each other's core values. This is about developing unity in the church leadership so that the effects trickle down and build a healthy culture in your entire church.

4. To all the women out there. This book is written using masculine pronouns in reference to the senior pastor and youth pastor. This was done just for the sake of readability. When I tried to write out things like "he or she" and "him or her" in every instance, the book became wordy and difficult to read. There are an equal number of women in leadership who are doing phenomenal jobs, and I fully intend to honor that. I wrote in this language solely for readability.

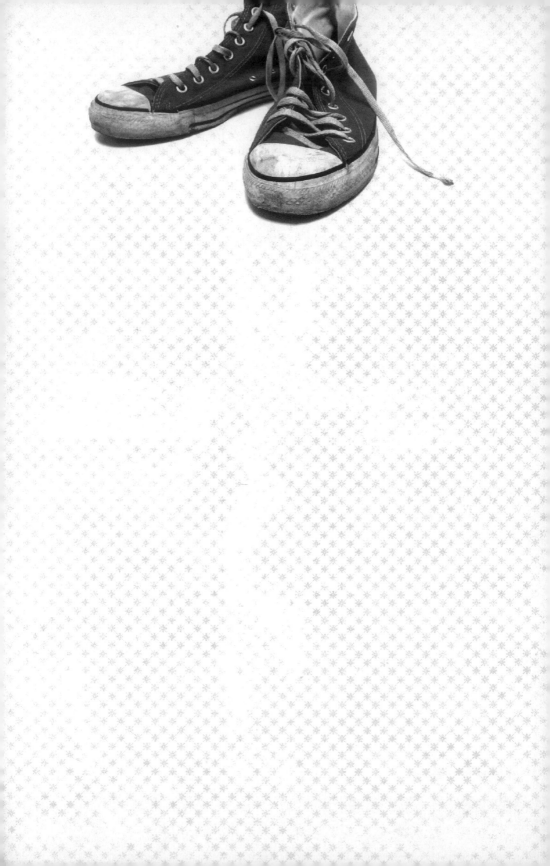

chapter 1

{ youth pastor }

What I Heard You Say Was...

Using communication that counts

There is so much that goes into having an effective, impactful youth ministry: discipling students, creating and running programs, managing a budget, leading and training adult volunteers, teaching transformationally, and last but not least, working with church staff. Bible college, internships, and seminary could never fully prepare anyone to handle your job. It requires you to wear many hats and communicate effectively in many situations. Not just the communication of your Wednesday night teaching or the counseling of a student, but also the small interactions in the office, the moments you're approached by parents or elders, the moments you're casting the vision to your volunteer staff, and especially the moments you're accountable to your senior pastor. Effective communication is a daily requirement for your job.

The easiest thing to do when we are busy or stressed (which seems to happen often in youth ministry) is to put our head down and just barrel through the work in front of us. We tend to communicate less frequently and effectively in stressful times. Most problems we face can be traced back to a breakdown in communication. Something was misunderstood, someone wasn't listening, or expectations weren't clear. The repercussions for these breakdowns can be huge.

Communication is the ingredient that will make or break your relationship with your senior pastor, your church and your ministry. Effective and clear communication can solve many problems before they even arise, and it has the ability to take your ministry and life forward in positive directions you never thought were possible.

> So many of the problems with communication lie in the fact that we just aren't honest with each other. For example, I do something as a youth pastor that makes the senior pastor go nuts, but instead of telling me, he goes and talks behind my back with a bunch of elders or other parents, and we never have an honest conversation about what frustrated him. Then I hear about it from some elder that is sent to "correct" me or "pacify" the senior pastor so that he can feel like I'm "handled."

Quality Over Quantity: Making It Intentional

Mark, the local youth pastor, worked hard at regularly communicating with his volunteers. They had calendars, expectations, and job descriptions. They even met once a month after church to talk about the next month and upcoming events. This surfaced great chaperones and helpers but didn't cultivate mentors of students—the greatest need of the ministry. Finally, after some advice from another youth pastor in town, Mark canceled the Sunday logistics meetings and turned the first 15 minutes of youth group every week into dodge-ball time. After the students showed up and had kicked off a game of dodge-ball, all the staff would go out in the hall to meet with Mark. Instead of sharing logistics and calendars with them, he would cast the vision of the youth ministry and the desire to see students transformed. He would then offer them one bit of advice or training to take and use as they built relationships with students that night, and then would send them off to do the transforming work.

This radically changed Mark's ministry. He had wanted mentors for the longest time but wasn't seeing any results. Yet after these small training sessions began, Mark noticed his adults begin to develop deeper relationships with students. He was also able to specifically challenge adults in these areas because his small trainings were addressing those issues. He was actually communicating less and having to prepare for less. But his communication was powerful and effective. It was intentional.

Speaking a lot of words, using body language, and listening aren't always enough. We can communicate until we are blue in the face, but unless it's intentional communication, it doesn't do much.

So much of our communication turns into bullet points or lists, getting lost in the white noise of church. This is especially true when we try to communicate to our senior pastors and others where our accountability is a factor. Our interactions with our senior pastors can often look like a student who's just returned from a life-changing mission trip. His parents ask him how the trip was and the student doesn't know what to say. He ends up going with "Great, Mom," or he fills in the silence with something both parties can understand: "The food was terrible" or "It rained every day while we were working" or even just "I loved working with the kids." When your senior pastor asks you how it's going, what do you say? Does your answer give him a clear view of the state of the youth ministry, or is it lost in the latest obstacle, funny story, or office detail? How intentional and focused is your communication with your senior pastor?

If you feel like your senior pastor doesn't understand what you're doing with the youth ministry or how students are growing, then try mixing up your traditional communication patterns with some of the following advice from other youth pastors. If your senior pastor doesn't buy in, he's less likely to support you when issues arise, help to provide extra resources, or provide you with the flexibility you desire.

> You know one of the biggest problems is the lack of time the senior pastor and youth pastor spend together. Senior pastors make all kinds of time to check youth pastors out when hiring them, but they make no time to sit with them and just see how they are doing. Communication works way better within a relationship. Giving or receiving communication from someone you don't know or who doesn't know you seems inauthentic.

Have 30-Second, 3-Minute, and 30-Minute Responses

Whether you have formal meetings or casual drop-ins, be ready for your senior pastor when he comes. Updating your senior pastor on the state of the youth ministry can be reduced to three responses: 30 seconds, 3 minutes, or 30 minutes. You should always be able to update your senior pastor based on these three response times. The key to developing these responses is knowing the ingredients, or formula, for each one. For a 30-second response, the formula looks like this:

big picture + the "why" + student growth = 30-second response

If you pass each other in the hall and he asks how it's going, have a 30-second response ready—"We are in the middle of our series on character, and the small group leaders are saying that students are starting to make some changes and growth steps in their integrity." You don't have much time, but you should be able to tell him the main theme in your ministry while also communicating the "why" behind it and the impact it is having on your students.

If your pastor has time, he might ask a few more questions about the ministry, offering a chance for your 3-minute response. For a 3-minute response, the formula looks like this:

big picture + the "why" + student growth + student story = 3-minute response

Having a 3-minute conversation gives you the opportunity to tell your senior pastor the big picture, communicate the "why," talk about your student growth, and also take it a step further by communicating a student story about what God is doing in or through them. This story adds a personal element to your overview conversation, and it lets the senior pastor know you are connecting with your students.

Every once in a while, you are given the opportunity to provide a 30-minute update on the youth ministry. This may come in a staff meeting or a one-on-one with the senior pastor. For a 30-minute response, the formula looks like this:

mission + short-term goals + strategic plan + impact + needs = 30-minute response

The key to the 30-minute response is your youth ministry's mission. Share with him in detail how every ministry within the youth group is doing on the mission. If you have small groups, go into detail about what is happening in the groups. Communicate your short-term goals within each ministry and how you are equipping your adult staff to work with students. You should also lay out your long-term strategic plan and the impact you hope the youth group will have in students' lives. This 30-minute update also offers the perfect opportunity to communicate your needs. Be very clear and realistic when you present your desires and how the church could help. Again, the main key of this conversation is communicating the youth ministry's mission. Make sure everything you say relates back to the mission so your senior pastor knows the "why" behind all you do. By having this 30-minute conversation already prepared, it also keeps you accountable to following through on your mission.

These three conversations may seem like a lot to prepare, but these small interactions hold huge power. Having these responses ready for your senior pastor builds his confidence in you and the youth ministry. It also arms the senior pastor for complaints or questions from other church members about the youth ministry. From these conversations, he knows that you have a strategic plan, effective small groups, capable staff, and positive outcomes. Arm your senior pastor any chance you can get. It will only grow the support for you and your ministry.

> **Isn't this messed up! You have to have these little presentations ready in your mind because the relationships are so rushed and disconnected that you don't just talk together regularly. Maybe I live in an ideal world, but even busy staff people should be getting together to build relationships and get on the same page. I wonder if Jesus' disciples had to have a 30-second update ready for their leader? Do we always have to give in to the culture, or can we shape a new kind of church culture where people actually have time for each other?**

Be the First to Deliver Bad News!

There are only a few things worse to a senior pastor than hearing bad news about the youth ministry from someone other than you. When this happens, his first reaction is likely to be that of distrust, or wondering why you were hiding what happened. It's hard to deliver bad news. And youth ministry lends itself to some bad news. Combine immature students with sugar and hormones, a handful of hovering parents, wacky games, and college-aged volunteers, and we all know you're going to have some bad news. You'll also have some life-changing kingdom moments. But they are probably coupled with some things like a hospital visit, broken relationships, or a run-in with a parent.

The best thing you can do when bad news comes is to be the first one in the senior pastor's office. When students make a bad decision and sneak out in the middle of the night on a retreat, just bring it up. If a parent overreacts and storms into the church office, it will go a lot better if the senior pastor is educated on the matter—not just better for you, but better for the church. The parent will know the church leaders are working together and are on the same page. They will also know there isn't much room for gossip or exaggeration. Even in the hardest moments, be the first one into your senior pastor's office. Your senior pastor truly desires open and honest communication about these things, so be forthcoming. It will take courage, but it will demonstrate your maturity and trustworthiness as a leader in the church.

I once ran a retreat in my first year as a youth pastor. I allowed some of my student leaders to pick out the movie for the weekend with some tight parameters. They brought me a movie called *Up the Creek*. It had no rating on the box, and they assured me it was this great comedy about a race down a river. In the first minute of the movie, the race was started by a girl who lifted her shirt and yelled, "Go!" I made the mistake of trying to keep this under wraps—that backfired big time and led to a giant parent meeting and a ton of questions. It would have been way better to just fess up when we got back from the retreat. I bet my senior pastor might have even laughed had I told him before the phone calls started from the parents.

Don't Report; Communicate

There is a difference between reporting and communicating. Reporting can be done through e-mails or newsletters and is usually full of facts and numbers. Communicating is getting down to the heart of the matter and offering the "why" behind your program. We often don't get beyond reporting when we meet with our senior pastor because he doesn't already have the information we're reporting on. So there's a simple solution to this problem: Leave a paper trail of your ministry logistics, even if you weren't asked for one.

Leave calendar, phone, and address information for all retreats and outings, along with event budgets and your overall strategic plan. Chances are that you have these details somewhere in your e-mail or computer. Make a copy and stick it into your senior pastor's mailbox or regularly e-mail him. Do this for two reasons: so that every meeting with your senior pastor doesn't turn into a time of transactional logistics, and so that your senior pastor will give you ministry freedom and the ability to take risks. Leaving a paper trail can turn your meetings into a time of powerful and necessary communication. You were both placed by God at your church; take advantage of it. *You have the ability to hold each other up, pray for each other and the church, and learn from each other when you meet.* Don't report; communicate. When you move your meetings from reporting into communication, you'll see your relationship begin to change.

Silence = Negative Assumptions

When communication is lacking, a lot of room is left for insecurities and doubts to creep in. People tend to assume the worst in the midst of silence. Your senior pastor may become unsure of the state of the ministry, wondering how invested you are or if something is wrong. When you don't regularly check in or interact with your senior pastor, he will most likely begin to assume there's a problem. The funny thing is we often don't check in when the ministry is doing really well because we don't need as much help. But that can actually hurt the situation more than help it. When things are great, check in with your senior pastor, and things likely will stay great longer!

Effective communication between you and your senior pastor is key to making your relationship work to the benefit of you, your ministry, and the whole church. When the two of you are in sync, there is not much that can tear you down. But it takes effort and hard work on your part to get to that point. Make it important, and your relationship will likely flourish.

The following activity is for you to assess the quality of your communication and see how intentional it is. There is a similar assessment for senior pastors in the first chapter of the senior pastor section of this book. Take the assessment on your own, and begin to make some small changes that will begin to transform the communication between you and your senior pastor.

Intentional Communication

Assessment

The following is an assessment to help determine how intentional your communication is with your senior pastor. While this assessment can be helpful, ultimately, you know best how you are communicating well and how you need to improve in the communication that you share.

If you are going through this book with your senior pastor, take 30 minutes this week to go through this activity on your own, and then meet with your senior pastor to discuss your thoughts. This assessment coincides with the senior pastor section of the book.

1. Are your meetings (aside from entire church staff meetings) spontaneous or planned?
   a. Always spontaneous
   b. Half and half
   c. Usually planned

2. What is your attitude going into a meeting with your senior pastor?
   a. I avoid it.
   b. I tolerate it.
   c. I have a positive attitude about it.

3. How well does your senior pastor know your ministry?
   a. He knows the ministry numbers.
   b. He knows the basic schedule of events.
   c. He knows the "why" behind the ministry and its greatest needs.

4. How well do you understand the pressures your senior pastor is facing?
   a. I think I know what they are, but I'm not certain.
   b. I am aware of the pressures he's facing.
   c. I offer support and pray for him as he faces these pressures.

5. How often do you feel that your senior pastor just doesn't get your approach to ministry?
   a. Very often. He just doesn't understand me or youth ministry.
   b. He sometimes gets it, but has too many other concerns.
   c. He asks good questions and tries hard to understand the youth ministry and me.

6. How well have you communicated the purpose behind your youth ministry programming?
   a. I give a report on what activities we are doing every year.
   b. I've laid out the youth ministry plan and a reason for each part of it.
   c. I regularly meet and share about why we are doing each of our programs, their impact and challenges.

7. How well do you know your senior pastor?
   a. I know a little about him and his approach to ministry.
   b. I know him on a personal level, and I'm beginning to understand what motivates him.
   c. I know him well, and his heart and dreams for ministry.

8. How much evaluation have you received from your senior pastor?
   a. We evaluate once a year, and when issues arise.
   b. We evaluate a few times a year, especially after an event.
   c. We regularly discuss my overall performance.

9. Do you know what "a job well done" looks like to your senior pastor?
   a. I am not sure what he considers "a job well done."
   b. I have an idea, but I had to learn it the hard way—through trial and error.
   c. I know what my senior pastor expects from me and what he considers a good job.

10. When my senior pastor and I meet, we communicate about
    a. Problems and concerns mostly.
    b. Logistics/calendar and problems.
    c. Our ministries' progress and needs, and personal life issues.

Add up your scores below.

A_____ B_____ C_____

Based on your scores, take a look at what category your communication fits into, and come up with an action plan that you can initiate this week to help make your communication more intentional.

A's = 2 or more and C's = 2 or less

If you had more than 2 A's and less than 2 C's, your communication with your senior pastor is not very intentional. It's probably lacking in both quality and quantity and could have some potential bitterness and judgments mixed up with it. This type of communication tends to lead toward negative assumptions by both parties and a natural division. Although you may be able to function together, you are not reaching the full potential of what a unified team in ministry can reach. Consider taking the following steps: First, begin praying specifically for your senior pastor daily. This can often change some of our own attitudes and understanding of someone. Second, ask for a time when you and your senior pastor can meet, and you can show him your strategic plan for the youth ministry, and the "why" behind each part of it (make sure to include your heart behind it). This will take time, and possibly several attempts, but it could open the door to a new type of communication and a new platform for your relationship.

Action Step:

A's = 1 or more and C's = 3 or less

If you had 1 or more A's and less than 4 C's, your communication with your senior pastor is somewhat regular but not as intentional as it could be. You have a foundation built on communication, but interactions are more transactional than they are intentional. Your communication has some necessary logistic and calendar focus but lacks in overall purpose and the "why" behind what you're doing or planning. Take some time to think through some 3-minute responses from the chapter, and use casual interactions to begin to share ministry wins and ministry needs. Turn "water-cooler conversations" into intentional sharing and listening that will grow your senior pastor's respect and trust in you.

Warning: Check your heart! Are you playing church office politics, or do you really care about your senior pastor?

Action Step:

A's = 0 and C's = 4 or more

If you had no A's and more than 4 C's, your communication has a strong foundation and is pretty intentional. Continue the road you are on, and grow your relationship by going out of the way to serve and support your senior pastor. Move into the level of "soul care." Offer a good mix of respect and encouragement. This will most likely lead to reciprocation and an even stronger, healthier relationship. Consider hanging out with your senior pastor in a social setting, such as at a ball game, or even asking your senior pastor to mentor you in ministry.

Action Step:

chapter 2

{ youth pastor }

Aretha Franklin Said It Best...

How core values can lead to respect

very church has a set of rules, both spoken and unspoken, setting a basic boundary for our leadership culture. Some of these may sound familiar:

- Do wear collared shirts.

- Don't lock up without straightening up the youth room first.

- Do come to staff meetings at least ten minutes early.

- Don't ever get a tattoo or piercing.

- Do run big decisions by the youth pastor first.

- Don't assume that a text is a communication to parents.

This set of rules governs not only what is permissible but also what is expected for each staff member. Yet each staff member's core values determines how he operates inside of those boundaries. Core values are a set of internal values hardwired into your DNA that act as a compass. Core values guide our behavior, affect our attitude, and influence our decisions on a daily basis. These rules, or personal guides, are extremely important to an individual. Violating someone's core values can strike a nerve, but respecting and encouraging them can be a catalyst for success, both in an individual's performance and in team unity.

Each person can only have a handful of core values. There are definitely more things that we value (and we should if we are following God's Word), but there are only a handful of principles that make up our gut reactions and natural inclinations. There are only a few things woven so deep in our core that it is extremely difficult for us to violate them. They are directly connected to our emotions, filling us with joy when we are in line with them and frustration when we can't live by them. Ultimately, it's not bad to have core values. In fact it's actually quite helpful for balance.

Here are some signifiers to indicate that team members are feeling like they are living out their own values on the job:

- They seem satisfied, not worn out.

- They are responsible and trustworthy; they don't drop balls or disappoint.

- They are connected to the overall mission and the team.

- They take appropriate risks because they are risking from a confident and fulfilled mind-set.

- They display and encourage positive attitudes.

Obviously, core values are important, but here's the daunting truth about core values: It is impossible to have a positive relationship with someone if you don't understand and respect their core values. Seriously, it's impossible. Unless we understand and respect people at their core, we will end up offending them or driving them away—sometimes without even knowing it. Failure to allow others to live out of their core values will only breed contempt and frustration.

Here are some signifiers to let you know when team members feel their values are being violated or they are unable to live them out on the job:

- They focus too much on small problems or on one issue.

- They becomes overly sensitive or touchy. They lack a sense of humor.

- They overreact to situations and become judgmental.

- They seem to be pushing their own agenda or viewpoint much of the time.

- They act frustrated with not being heard or give off the impression that they are outsiders.

 These are great relational insights, far beyond the senior pastor/youth pastor relationship!

People are generally pretty good at determining what's really important to someone and what doesn't matter much. But how can you use this skill to build a strong relationship with your senior pastor?

Take a look at two scenarios that many churches experience when it comes to core values.

1. The senior pastor has the core value of evangelism, and the youth pastor has the core value of discipleship. The church mission statement includes evangelism, discipleship, and service, but the major emphasis of church life is clearly evangelism. Evaluations and meetings center around evangelism and success is gauged by numbers of new attendees. But the youth ministry is discipleship oriented because the youth pastor has the core value of shepherding. Small groups are where most of the time and budget are spent for the youth ministry, with their primary focus on spiritual growth, not outreach.

Both the senior pastor and youth pastor are living out the church mission, but tension between them is growing. The youth pastor doesn't feel like his ministry is valued and isn't encouraged unless a new family comes to church via the youth ministry. And the senior pastor wonders why the youth pastor is trying to run a "separate" church within the church. Distance grows between them, and other staff even begin to take sides. Instead of deep listening and understanding, they begin to manipulate and tolerate each other until it takes a toll on their leadership and on the church.

2. The senior pastor has the core value of achievement, and the youth pastor has the core value of community. The church is known for being on the forefront of growth and new ideas. Decisions are made quickly, and things are always moving forward. The youth pastor struggles in this environment because it feels like systems matter more than people. Every staff meeting makes the youth pastor feel like a train just ran over him, and he has a growing disdain for new ideas. More than getting things accomplished, the youth pastor cares about the state of the team, team members' relationships, and how they are feeling.

The youth pastor and senior pastor collide on this, often creating more distance. The senior pastor feels like the youth pastor disrespects him and is causing roadblocks to growth. Their relationship is fragile at best, and even the smallest thing turns into angry frustration.

> This is a very realistic example—although details are often different, the underlying core value conflict is omnipresent.

In both of these situations, and probably in most situations, the problem is not that each person has different core values. It's that they don't understand, offer grace, or respect each other's values.

A lot of the difficulties in a youth pastor/senior pastor relationship could be avoided if both understood each other's core values. However, knowing each other's core values is oftentimes not enough. Here are some ways that you can make core values a point of connection in your relationship with your senior pastor.

Identify Core Values

At the end of this chapter, you (and your senior pastor, I hope) will go through an exercise that will help you put a name to your core values. As part of that exercise, you will also try to identify your senior pastor's core values. To help you do this, go back through the signifiers in the previous section and see which ones apply to him. Start writing down what you think might be some of his core values.

Get to Know the "Why" Behind the Values

A person's values are formed in many different ways. Here are three common sources for values:

- An influential person in his life

- A part of Scripture that means a lot to him

> Scripture is sometimes a common source, but more often I see it as a spiritual experience—which may include Scripture, or prayer, or a mission trip, or camp—a turning point.

- Life experiences—good and bad

When you peel back the layers to an emotional response, it often comes back to one of these three sources.

Don't Label Values as "Old School"

Many youth pastors come into their churches and are the youngest members of the staff. Chances are they walk into a system that is well established and deeply ingrained. The youth pastor has a great opportunity to bring a fresh perspective and offer a voice from outside the system. But even though the system might be "old school," the values behind it are very real and very current to your senior pastor. As you desire to make changes to the system, make sure that your changes still take into account the core values of the old system and your teammates. You are more likely to make lasting change when you identify that the new idea is backed by the same core values.

Appreciate Others' Core Values

It's easy to look at life just through the lens of our own core values. If focus is a big deal for you, then you may get impatient with a lot of relational time with seemingly no clear purpose. If discipline or routine is a high value, a staff member who values spontaneity and flexibility may frustrate you. Expecting people to have the same core values will only disappoint you. I'm not saying that your values are wrong or unbiblical, but the extremity to which you desire to live them out is not realistic for every person. They can't live out your core values any more than you can adopt and passionately live out theirs. The answer? Offer grace. Other people are wired differently, and it's a good thing. You and your church need a diversity of gifts and passions to minister effectively.

Make Room for Your Senior Pastor's Values

Yes, your senior pastor's values are likely different than yours. They may even be frustrating or disheartening. But when your senior pastor is living out his core values, he will be more content and satisfied. In that state of mind, he is also more likely to positively face change, dream, and have an open mind. Make room in your expectations, time, judgments, and conversations for your senior pastor to live out his values. It will benefit him, you, and the church.

Adopt One of Your Senior Pastor's Core Values for a Week

Give it a shot. If productivity is one of his core values, see how many things you can accomplish from start to finish this week. If innovation is a core value, set aside some time each day to look at your ministry and ask, "Is there a better way?" If family time is a value, add a family night into your programming. Do this to experience the benefits of your senior pastor's core values and to gain a deeper understanding of what drives his passion for ministry.

 What a cool idea!

Getting in tune with your senior pastor's core values will make or break your relationship and your ministry. When you are honoring your senior pastor's core values and not imposing your values on him, your relationship will grow. Here are some results from this that could possibly emerge:

- You will be given more ministry freedom.

- Your senior pastor will be less likely to micromanage.

- You will be the first choice for new responsibilities or endeavors.

- Your senior pastor will be more eager to listen to your ministry plans.

- Encouragement will become more frequent and natural.

- There will be less manipulation or passive-aggressive behavior.

- Your senior pastor will be more aware of your needs.

When we live by our core values, we tend to be at our best. We fire on all cylinders. But when they are not honored, we tend to be at our worst. Our life and ministry seem off balance. The following is an activity to do on your own, and then

Discovering Core Values

Profile

compare it with your senior pastor's, if possible, to identify your respective core values and to gain an understanding of the "why" behind them.

On pages 29-30, you will find a list of 81 different core values. This list will serve as the basis for helping you discover your core values. As you glance down the page, you may decide that in some way or another, you actually value every item on the list. While that may be true, know that the point of the exercise is to unearth the few values that are absolutely essential to who you are and how you were created. This will be a challenge, as true self-discovery always is. But if you take this exercise seriously, it will help you understand more concretely your mode of operation.

If you are going through this book with your senior pastor, take 30 minutes this week to go through this activity on your own, and then meet with your senior pastor to discuss your thoughts. This assessment coincides with the senior pastor section of the book.

IMPORTANT! Complete each step before moving on to the next one.

1. As you read each core value listed at the end of this chapter, decide whether you would consider it **somewhat important** in your day-to-day life or **important**. If you consider it to be **somewhat important**, draw a line through the word, crossing it out. Go through the whole list using this approach. Do not give too much thought to your choices, go with your first reaction.

2. Once you've completed this first step, go back through the list once again, only reading the words that are **not** crossed out. As you read each core value listed, decide in your head whether you would consider it **important** in your day-to-day life or **very important**. If you consider it to be **important**, draw a line through the word, crossing it out. Go through the whole list using this approach.

3. Once you've completed this second step, go back through the list once again, only reading the words that are not crossed out. As you read each core value listed, decide whether you would consider it **very important** in your day-to-day life or **extremely important**. If you consider it to be **very important**, draw a line through the word, crossing it out. Go through the whole list using this approach.

4. Repeat this whole process until you have narrowed the list down to no more than three to five core values that are **extremely important** to you.

Now that you've completed the search for your core values, it's time to ask yourself some key questions regarding these values and how they play into your life.

Where did your core values come from?

Core values tend to originate from three main sources: influential people, meaningful Scripture verses, and significant life experiences. Take some time to examine each of the core values you've discovered, and ask yourself where its existence stems from in your life. Knowing the origin helps you and others understand the core value's presence in your life.

_____

_____

_____

_____

Why do each of these values remain important to you?

Knowing where your values come from is not enough; it's imperative to also understand why these values are extremely significant in your life today. Spend a few moments and go through each value, taking time to think about why the value remains important in your life today.

_____

_____

_____

_____

How do my core values affect my ministry?

This is a very significant question and is extremely pertinent to the discussion with your senior pastor. Your core values deeply affect the way you run your ministry and the way you perceive value within the ministry. Go through your core values and write down how you see your values affecting the ministry you lead.

What are your senior pastor's core values?

After working alongside your senior pastor for weeks, months, and years, it may seem abundantly clear to you the core values present in your senior pastor's life. Write down what values you think are central to your senior pastor and how you see these values lived out on a regular basis.

How can you help?

In ministry, as in life, respecting another person's core values is key to maintaining an intentional relationship. Think of ways that you can personally show significance to your senior pastor through his core values and maybe even raise the level to which you value those qualities.

Discipleship	Mentoring	Community	Evangelism
Influencing Others	Safety/Security	Knowledge/Learning	Personal Freedom
Cooperation/Teamwork	Variety	Understanding	Hard Work
Tolerance	Risk Taking	Winning	Faith
Family	Hope	Initiative	People
Productivity	Achievement	Control	Pioneering
Beauty	Balance	Unity	Change
Authenticity	Consistency/Dependability	Decency	Gratitude
Fun	Fulfillment	Friendships/Relationships	Experiences
Empowerment	Creativity	Concern for Individuals	Simplicity
Success	Competence	Truth	Transformation
Love	Challenge	Excellence/Quality	Generosity
Forgiveness	Potential	Compassion/Mercy	Opportunity
Self-Renewal	Intimacy	Significance	Innovation
Impact	Trust	Time/Freedom	Purity
Responsibility	Respect	Purpose	Integrity
Honesty	Power	Prayer	Character

Sensitivity	Self-Worth	Duty	Perseverance
Loyalty	Courage	Prestige/ Reputation	Money/Wealth
Joy	Kindness	Perfection	Humility
Shepherding			

chapter 3

{ youth pastor }

Ministry Is Where the Money Is...

If that were true, we wouldn't have this chapter

nce money gets mixed in with ministry, things can get very messy. There are some healthy ways we should treat and handle it, but there are some unhealthy realities that can exist in our churches, solely because we are broken people. The goal of this chapter is to encourage and prepare you for an honest conversation with your senior pastor that helps the two of you understand the financial pressure and stress you're facing, as well as understand how each of you interprets "value."

Sometimes these conversations need to be had with their supervisors instead of senior pastors. In some churches, the senior pastor does not have any say regarding budgets or salaries. So youth pastors may need to have these conversations with their executive or department heads.

We Equate Money With Value

When the youth ministry doesn't get a significant portion of the church budget but the tech team or the children's ministry does, you might feel like the church doesn't value the ministry that you've devoted your life to. It can make you feel misunderstood or unwilling to listen or change when a staff member brings up the fact that the youth seem separate from the rest of the church. It may create division leading to disunity and eventually puts in our minds the plague of "I deserve." You focus on the idea that the youth ministry deserves more money, more time, more support, more value, and so on. As soon as that plague comes upon us, our perspective can change from a kingdom perspective to a selfish one that treats the other staff and the rest of the church poorly. Manipulation, judgment, and sour feelings can rear their ugly heads.

Money is a sensitive subject. So let's look at some of the common ways it affects youth ministries and youth workers, and the workers' relationship with their senior pastors. My hope is that this may help prevent problems and keep us off of the road of "I deserve."

Remembering the Source

If you work at Starbucks, it is clear what the source of your income is: coffee. After your barista training, serving thousands of drinks, cleaning bathrooms, and smelling like coffee every night, you look at your paycheck and think, "Nice. Forty hours in this paycheck. Paid for by coffee."

Ministry work is more complex. Ultimately, we know God is the source of all our provisions. But practically speaking, it is people who sacrifice and give that pay for pastors to be able to receive a salary and provide programming. Many of the people in your congregation, like you, are struggling to survive—some of them have lost their jobs, have financial crunches, or family tragedies. But they still give.

> This needs to be remembered when we get so frustrated and we speak to leaders and parents in our ministry about "lack" of resources. We can ruin our ability to minister to others by voicing our bitterness over the issue.

It's humbling to think about and, in a healthy way, keeping this in mind helps us to have a kingdom perspective.

Our attitudes about money have the potential to destroy us and destroy our ministries. Remembering that the resources we have been given come from God and the generosity of people can be a lifeline that keeps bitterness and judgment at bay. This reality is the weapon we use to fight against the attitudes of entitlement, bitterness, and half-heartedness.

Another reality of working in a role that is funded by donations is that your stewardship has more immediate consequences and is watched by those who give. This creates a sense of responsibility that can be healthy, and cause us to really think carefully before we use our credit cards (church or personal). Now, that doesn't mean you shouldn't buy pizza for a small group or take students to a water park. These can be powerful ministry opportunities. But it does mean that you feel the responsibility of being a steward of the church community's resources.

> How you invest or are perceived to invest the church's money will be a factor to your ministry receiving more.

The Church Budget

It has been said that if you want to know what is important to someone, check his bank statement and daily planner. How a person spends time and money will tell you where the priorities really lie. It's the same for churches. The mission statement and the pastor's pursuits are really just a small part of the story. The annual budget will tell more about a church's mission than the sign hung on the wall.

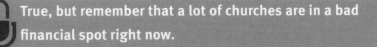

As you enter a church budget meeting to make your case for the youth ministry, there's a lot going through the minds of the decision makers in that room. They are remembering encounters they've had with students, the condition of the youth room, the nicks and dents in the church vans, and any retreat or ski trip debacle! Your job is not to defend less-than-perfect moments, but to give an explanation of the values behind your spending. Your youth ministry budget is a reflection of your mission and values. Express that.

Give the "why" for everything you do in youth ministry. It may seem obvious to you that the ski trip is the main outreach-focused event of the youth ministry, but that may not be obvious to the budget setters. Give the "why" behind every budget request you make, and live up to the "why" all year long as you spend that budget.

It will help you to have an advocate in the room who understands what you want to accomplish or the mission of your ministry. If you don't have someone like that in the room, invite someone to your ministry—take him out to talk about what your hopes and dreams are.

You may be viewed as a "risk taker." The decision makers are looking at your track record to see if you, your vision, and your ability to execute are worthy of extra dollars.

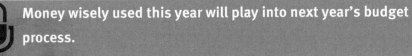

Money wisely used this year will play into next year's budget process.

Salary

A minister's salary is one of the hardest topics to address in the church. As a youth pastor, we may feel "devalued"—squeezed by the church to get the most work out of us for the least amount of money. Inside we are conflicted. We believe that ministry should be a sacrifice, so we try and dismiss or balance our negative thoughts with things like

- I should be content, no matter what.

- It's all part of sacrifice.

- It's wrong for me to ask for more pay.

- I don't have a retirement or college plan for my kids, but there are people starving in the world, so I should be happy.

Covering over our frustrations and feelings with these statements will not make us feel more valued. If you don't address your feelings properly, they may lead you into low performance, entitlement, and a dislike for certain church members. Long term, the best thing you can do is come up with a budget that soundly and specifically describes your needs in providing for you and your family. When you have this plan—one that includes things like retirement, health insurance, and savings—you can then begin making personal choices and setting personal goals for achieving them.

Many times, we suspect that we don't make enough, but we don't know how much we need or the steps we need to take in order to be fiscally responsible. A specific plan, with dollar amounts attached, is a great tool for your senior pastor and elders to use to begin helping you strategically provide for your family and future. Often churches have a finance committee or executive pastor who handles this. Our churches are often full of experienced business leaders and financial advisers. Take advantage of their skills by asking a trusted person to become your financial mentor.

 Take the course on financial advice that your church offers, such as Crown Financial Ministries or Financial Peace University.

Look for someone who can help you plan well, offer wise counsel, and maybe even advocate for you. If you are struggling financially, your church may not even know it. This person can help mediate and advocate as an outside party.

A couple of things to consider:

- Going more than three years without a raise is not common.

- Your church may not know about your needs unless you tell them. Your church is more likely to support and sustain you if you have a practical plan.

- Raises shouldn't always come with more responsibility; it's not a raise if you are just working more hours.

WARNING: Be worthy of your salary. Don't ask for more if you've squandered what you've been given. Your stewardship is the most important factor here.

> A lot of churches use ranges for each position. They have done research that tells them where you are in the range. Ask for that information. They may have not factored in all the relevant details of your situation. If they did a national range search, it will feel low if you are living in an area where the cost of living is higher. Understanding how they make their decisions will help you have an eloquent conversation about your pay.

I've Paid My Dues!

Always remember that a church's staff structure may look slightly different from a secular corporation. The time and work the senior pastor has put in this year must be put in perspective with the time and work he has put in over the past 10 or 20 years, building the foundation of his leadership. He has traveled a long road to get where he is now—not just financially, but in influence, relationships, decision-making freedoms, and less instances of people looking over his shoulder.

Your senior pastor may not be asked to log hours now, but it still may be required of you. Your senior pastor may be given freedoms that you are not given. Your senior pastor will probably get fewer budget questions, fewer "where were you" questions, and fewer theological questions after preaching a sermon. Your senior pastor probably receives a larger salary and budget than you do. This is not an injustice! His past ministry investment, experiences, and efforts are highly valuable. A wise church will also value your influence and perspective—but probably not right away. Trust is given over time. So is acceptance.

> This is true. You are evaluated based on your ability to be a team player and how well you make decisions with the money you are given.

This does not mean your senior pastor should take advantage of his situation. But you will end up miserable if you compare your freedoms to those of your senior pastor or other, more experienced church veterans.

Remember: Your pastor's freedom as perceived by you may not be accurate. I had a lot more freedom as a youth pastor than in the role I have now.

Your senior pastor also may translate it as disrespect when you challenge, compare, or question the situation.

Problems that emerge between senior pastors and youth pastors often stem from the root issue of respect. And the long road that the senior pastor has been walking is something very personal, and he might have low tolerance for a challenge. But if you feel you must challenge him on something, be careful and *always* do it with respect.

Go out of your way to respect your senior pastor's efforts. Don't ignore them because you feel disrespected. Your respect toward him will grow your humility. Go out of your way this week to encourage and acknowledge your senior pastor's journey and investment, and watch your relationship begin to change.

Take some time to go through the following exercise to evaluate the ways money and your perspective of money influence your ministry. If possible, meet with your senior pastor after he goes through his section, and debrief together. Imagine how powerful your team can be if you are completely unified and genuinely concerned for each other. And if you are on a strong, supportive team, use this experience as a way to exercise extra care for each other this week.

Money Perceptions

Assessment

If you are going through this book with your senior pastor, take 30 minutes this week to go through this activity on your own, and then meet with your senior pastor to discuss your thoughts. This assessment coincides with the senior pastor section of the book.

Take some time and respond to the following questions.

How much stress does money or things related to money put on you?

1	2	3	4	5	6	7	8	9	10

None   It's overwhelming

How much stress does money or things related to money put on your family relationships?

1	2	3	4	5	6	7	8	9	10

None   It's overwhelming

How well do you feel like you are managing your personal finances?

1	2	3	4	5	6	7	8	9	10

Not very well   Very well

Is your attitude positive or negative toward your church when it comes to matters of money?

1	2	3	4	5	6	7	8	9	10

Negative   Positive

What specific challenges are you facing in your personal life financially?

How are you doing with debt? What is your debt situation?

How much financial planning have you done for your future (yes, even if you're single)? This includes retirement, kids' college, and investments.

What is the lack of money keeping you from doing in your ministry? Be specific.

How often do you pray about the financial pressures of the church?

How easy or difficult is tithing for you? Why?

Based on your answers, what warning signs or areas do you see that need to change (such as attitude, tithing, stewardship)? Take a minute to write down why that area is a problem for you, and spend some time confessing it.

Now take a minute to write down some growth steps to how you plan on changing this problem area in your life starting this week.

Example: I'm going to write out a check every Sunday (not once a month or online) for my tithe. I will begin to make this an act of worship in my life.

chapter 4

{ youth pastor }

I Wanted a Cadillac, but I Got a Chevy...

Aligning your expectations

**Y**ou and your kids are available to help us in the nursery again, right? I know you are having your all-nighter on Friday, but this could be a great start to the night! Now you can weave service into the night. It's perfect! Remember, we'll need you here from 6 until 10. Oh, and don't be late, Doug. The last time we needed your help, most of your kids were late, and it messed everything up."

It was happening again. Third time in the last four months to be exact. I was backed into a corner by my senior pastor and pretty much told what to do. You see, whenever the adult ministries wanted to put on an event at my church, it was automatically assumed the students in the youth ministry would do the baby-sitting. It never mattered that we had an event during that same time or even in the same space, because if the adults needed something, the students were there to serve them. My youth group members became second-class citizens, expected by most, including the pastor, to baby-sit whenever needed. It's not that my students didn't like baby-sitting; in fact, many of them loved it and regularly baby-sat for the congregation. They would have gladly done it with joyful hearts had they simply been asked. But it wasn't like that. They were instead told and expected to push all their other plans aside. I dreaded this conversation every time and hated the unrealistic expectations shoved onto me and my students.

We've all had expectations placed on us before, whether it's by parents or our senior pastor. Truth is, we can't help but have expectations. They are innate assumptions formed out of past experiences, relationships, and future hopes. They began the first time we cried as a baby—someone gave us food, and we knew if we cried, we could expect to be fed. We form expectations for ourselves and for everyone around us. However, when our expectations are unrealistic or unfair, frustration and disappointment soon follow.

No matter how many sources you drew from to try and form accurate and realistic expectations about your job as a youth pastor, there is no way to pin down exactly what your senior pastor expects from you. He is drawing from his own experiences, relationships with past youth pastors, and future hopes. And to be honest, his expectations have a great deal to do with your job experience. It works both ways.

> Your senior pastor is likely to disappoint you because there is no way anyone can live up to the extreme amount of preconceived notions we have about church life, leadership, decision making, mentoring, and other relevant topics.

The goal of this chapter is to help you align expectations between you and your senior pastor and help uncover unrealistic ones on both sides of the table. Expectations that aren't aligned will only grow tension and create a void between you.

Uncover Your Church's History

There is a story that started long before you showed up on the scene. The last youth pastor that served at your church wrote a huge part of it, and upon his departure, real expectations were probably voiced. Uncover what your church leadership and senior pastor really appreciated and what they wish was different about the last youth pastor. Ask probing questions of all the church staff members and listen deeply to their responses.

This is so true. Remember that you are going into a culture of ministry, not just a neutral ministry context. Spend the time to interview the church as much as they interview you!

Chances are, expectations of you were forged through the previous youth pastor's story—both in ways people wish you would perform just like that person and ways that people wish you would be different. Gather all the info you can, and see if the "why" behind instructions given you becomes clear. This will directly influence your vision and mission statement because the "why" is what you will explain to parents, students, and staff. It makes sense then to understand the "why" of what you're getting into. Also, be willing to offer grace for some of the expectations placed on you because of the past. There are probably a lot of emotions tied up there.

If you are the first youth pastor ever at your church, look to the past to tell you what came to a boiling point that caused the church to hire you. Yes, there was obviously a need for the youth to be cared for, but there's likely more to the story. Was it out of exasperation? Volunteers had run themselves ragged, and you are the church's answer to handle it all. Was it because every other church had one? This creates an expectation to look or operate like another organization. Was it because some of the core youth were getting into major trouble, and you are "expected" to bring them out of it? Look at all the motives behind your hire to understand possible unspoken expectations.

If your senior pastor is new or has not been at your church long, you have a unique opportunity. The past that you look into will be that of your senior pastor's last church. Ask him what his relationship was like with the youth pastor, what the youth program looked like, and how they communicated best. You have an opportunity to lay a solid foundation with the senior pastor if you set the stage for aligning expectations and clear communication right away. Get to know what he expects, and be clear about your intentions.

Be Honest About Expectations You Can't Meet

You know your giftings, strengths, and passions more than anyone else. If expectations outside of your job description are distracting you or hampering your ministry, you must confront them. Letting them fester will only grow the problem into something unmanageable. Be honest with your senior pastor about the pressure this is causing. Take some time with him to point out where you see these expectations rising, and the effect it's having on your ministry. Most likely your senior pastor wants to hear your struggles and work through them with you. Do this sooner than later, before it costs more than you can give.

What Do You Expect From Your Senior Pastor?

Take a look at the following questions, and write down your answers on the lines below.

Do you dread or have a negative attitude toward meetings led by your senior pastor? Why? What would make those meetings better? How would you like your senior pastor to lead them differently?

Do you compare or wish your senior pastor was more like another pastor you know? What expectations of your relationship with him does this uncover (if any)?

Are you often critical of your senior pastor's sermons? Why? Is it the content, delivery, or his character that you are struggling with? What expectations of your senior pastor's teaching does this uncover (if any)?

What role do you desire your senior pastor to take in your development and growth professionally, personally, spiritually, etc.? What are your expectations of his availability to you as part of his staff versus other congregants and leaders?

Do you find yourself venting, grumbling, or even tactfully complaining to anyone else (including best friends or spouse) about your senior pastor? What is most frustrating to you? What might this uncover about your desires to be lead in certain ways?

In your mind, do you ever find yourself making excuses for your senior pastor? In what areas? What expectations is he not meeting?

 There is a fine balance here though of publicly showing loyalty to your senior pastor. Remember: public loyalty = private leverage!

What recent situations do you wish your senior pastor handled differently? What would you have done in those situations? What actions do you expect him to take that he's not taking?

When you look at your responses above, cross out any expectations that are obviously unrealistic. Next, put a star by the ones that are "do or die"—they must be met or you can't work there anymore. Now take a look at the rest of the expectations on the lines, and cross out the ones that you don't uphold yourself.

Based on the ones that remain, does your senior pastor know that you expect these from him? (If not, there will be a chance in the activity at the end of the chapter for you both to discuss them.) Based on the ones that you crossed out, what is the cost of holding your senior pastor to these (time, frustration, relationship, and so on)? What will you do to offer grace, and let go of the expectations that are unrealistic or that you can't even uphold yourself? Do you need to modify any of them? confess any? or change your own life to meet some of them?

Anytime we make excuses, vent, dream of a better day, compare, or dread, there's a good chance that we have an expectation that's not being met. We may slowly grow a divide with him in our hearts if we don't deal with these expectation issues. Either we end up extremely disappointed and frustrated, or we end up disenchanted and disengaged by releasing our expectations altogether. Dealing with them can mean communicating them directly to him in a gentle and appropriate way; or letting go of them and offering grace in the situation.

Remember: Most senior pastors are under the tremendous pressure of people's expectations to be perfect and all things to all people. He needs your support and understanding as much or more than anyone you know.

Expectations

Evaluation

Go through the following three steps, and work through how expectations are affecting your relationship with your senior pastor.

If you are going through this book with your senior pastor, take 30 minutes this week to go through this activity on your own, and then meet with your senior pastor to discuss your thoughts. This evaluation coincides with the senior pastor section of the book.

1. **Job Description**
   Pull out your job description. (It might be yellowing from sitting in a file for so long!)

   - On the bottom of the page, write down anything that has been added since it was written (officially added, not just things that have morphed into your routine).

   - Cross out any items that are no longer relevant, such as you used to oversee the children's ministry, but the church has since hired a director for that role.

   - Now go through each item on the page and label it accordingly.

     - F = Fulfilling

     - C = Cannot fulfill (this one is something that is out of your control, such as the church wanted you to do a youth mission trip, but this year they canceled it because of budget reasons)

     - N = Not fulfilling.

   Look at the job description after your labeling. How have you done at meeting the expectations given to you by the church? Are there any changes you need to make in order to meet these expectations?

2. **History and Culture**
   Make a list of expectations you think are placed on you by others in the church because of the church's past experiences, culture, and policies.

   Circle the ones on the list that you believe your senior pastor in particular expects you to fulfill. Are the circled expectations ones that will help you grow and build your relationship with your senior pastor, or are they ones that will burn you out and create disunity in your relationship? What changes do you need to make to keep from burning out or allowing disunity to creep into your relationship? Write down your thoughts to these questions and talk with your senior pastor, and together make a plan that can keep you from burnout and disappointment.

3. **Unrealistic Expectations**

On page 48, you narrowed down a list of expectations you have for your senior pastor. This week, focus on this list. If you are getting frustrated or judgmental, ask yourself if it fits into one of the expectations you had on your list, and if not, let it go! It's not worth it, and it will only lead to unhealthy reactions. Focus hard on giving grace. Give up gossip, judgment, and unrealistic expectations. If it is a realistic expectation, confront it. Otherwise, let it go.

chapter 5

{ youth pastor }

Getting Off the Elevator on the Same Floor...

What a shared mission can do for you

It's not that hard for a youth ministry to become an entity of its own—or a "little church." In fact, this approach is inherited. It starts in the church nursery, then into the children's ministry, to middle school, and finally into high school. When the teens in your youth group were seven years old, they probably functioned inside of the children's ministry, without really knowing what's going on in the rest of the church. They may have joined their family in the adult worship service for the beginning (during the music) but then were whisked away to a "kid-friendly" service (typically before the pastor's sermon). But in middle and high school, that perspective changes. The expectation of most churches becomes that the students must begin to integrate into the "adult" world of the church, but still maintain separate programming.

Regardless of where this approach originated, take a minute to consider the divide that often exists between youth ministries and "big church." Typically, youth ministry is the segment of the church that most reflects the processes and programs of the church as a whole (small groups, discipleship, sermon/teaching, service projects, mission trips, evangelism, worship) while still being separate from the "big church." The youth ministry often has its *own* small groups and its *own* worship times, and often its *own* space in the church, too.

Many people in church leadership will point to separate programming as the reason why the youth are disengaged from the rest of the church. Inevitably, there will be some form of a divide between most youth ministries and the other ministries of their churches, a chasm that often rips churches apart. Here's the thing: T*he problem is not the divide* (at least not in the way you think).

The problem is not so much the physical and programmatic division, but the *division from the mission.* When the youth ministry (or any ministry for that matter) veers off in its own direction away from the church's original mission, chaos ensues. When the mission gets divided, so do the staff, the resources, the parents, and the givers of resources. A unified mission and vision are lost as ministries strive to reach their own audience in their own, individual way. Silos are formed and walls are built causing competition and relational strain.

For all of you William Wallace fans out there, remember at the end of *Braveheart* (if you have not seen the movie, I am about to spoil the ending for you) when Wallace is tortured by being literally yanked in two separate directions? It hurts my whole body just to think about this. His muscles, joints, organs, and nervous system were stretched to the breaking point. Even before it cost him his life, Wallace's body lost the ability to function. Joints were yanked out of their sockets, muscles spasmed and twisted. While gruesome, this picture is what it's like for a church on two separate missions. It's torture. Every resource, staff, system, and member is stretched to the point of dysfunction.

So what's the difference between being divided by program and space, and being divided by mission? Well, ultimately one will cost the church, while the other will be a catalyst for the church. And while a diversion from the mission can be subtle and creep up on a church, many steps can be taken to avoid it ever taking root.

Divisive Talk

Do you, your leaders, or other staff members ever say things like...

"The 'big boys' upstairs want us to change this now."

"The 'mother ship' has called a meeting next week."

"My students don't like going to 'big church.' "

Usually when we start talking like this, it's because we consider ourselves a separate entity from the rest of the church. It's a sign of a disconnected culture and disloyalty. It plays out in everyday actions and everyday conversations.

Youth pastor Andrew is talking with his assistant and discipleship leaders about an upcoming youth event. They've decided to do a fall fest and want to cart bales of hay into the newly built sanctuary. The assistant suddenly asks a probing question: "Do you think they'll care if we pile a bunch of hay into the sanctuary?" Everyone stops for a second to think but eventually laughs it off, with Andrew pointing out that in this case, "It's better to ask for forgiveness than for permission." As the discussion moves on, one of the boys' discipleship leaders asks if anyone got the latest memo from the "guys upstairs." "Even though they cut our budget so every office would have new glass doors installed for liability sake, they've now mandated that we can never have our doors completely shut. They must always be open at least 6 inches. How ridiculous is that!"

This church obviously has some big problems—disloyalty being one of them. It's obvious from their conversation they are divided from the mission, and their words only fuel the disloyalty in their hearts. Disloyalty is a slow and subtle process, weaving its way into a person's mind until it's all they focus on. In 2 Samuel 15:2-6, King David's own son Absalom used his words so powerfully yet so subversively to undermine his father's reign. He knew what he was doing. His words and actions spread disloyalty and divided the kingdom. The people of Israel in time put their trust in him, and David temporarily lost his throne.

He got up early every morning and went out to the gate of the city. When people brought a case to the king for judgment, Absalom would ask where in Israel they were from, and they would tell him their tribe. Then Absalom would say, "You've really got a strong case here! It's too bad the king doesn't have anyone to hear it. I wish I were the judge. Then everyone could bring their cases to me for judgment, and I would give them justice!"

When people tried to bow before him, Absalom wouldn't let them. Instead, he took them by the hand and kissed them. Absalom did this with everyone who came to the king for judgment, and so he stole the hearts of all the people of Israel.

> This is so common and it kills the church staff. We too quickly jump to conclusions. We need to trust people and offer grace rather than disdain. We would be wise to follow Jesus' words in Matthew 18 when confronting a problem between staff members.

The same can happen in a church. Somewhere along the way, the mission of the church isn't clearly communicated, and it gets taken for granted. It becomes easy for many different people with many different agendas to go their own way. Just imagine if everyone in your church got to declare and make the decisions about the mission of the church. Insurance agents, college students, bonds salesmen, stay-at-home moms—all interpreting and casting a vision for the rest of the church. Pretty soon disloyalty would reign, and no one would lead the church. A lot of work goes into undoing a divided mission, but a good start is in changing your language. When we communicate disloyalty, we pour fuel on the fire of division.

Your influence can perpetuate or diffuse the problem. When church leaders know they are respected, they are more likely to respect you. So be mindful of the way you speak, for once the language changes, hearts will change also.

Focus on Families

You and your senior pastor both serve families (taking into account, of course, that you both serve God first, and serving families is an outflow of that). It can be easy to compartmentalize church ministries by age or affiliation, but when families leave individual ministries in church, they go back to the same home. Children, teenagers, parents, and grandparents are all in this together.

If you are running an effective youth ministry and creating students who own their faith, it will help the whole family. And likewise, if your senior pastor is able to equip parents to develop their children into disciples of Christ, while at the same time edifying their spouses, it will help the whole family. Success in each area of ministry only helps and builds a strong platform for every other ministry. Focus on the people you and your senior pastor serve. You are on the same mission—to effectively serve families. Edify, support, defend, and pick up slack for each other. Don't take this lightly, and don't trade it for anything. Stay on the same mission.

Never Create Your Calendar in Isolation

It's common for each department in a church to make its own calendar of events. And as these events pop up, other departments are often put in defense mode. Everyone competes for the church's resources (vans, space, parents' time, and so on), and the attitude begins to take the form of "What can I get?" rather than "What can I give?"

Choose to collaborate as you plan your calendar. Show a mock-up to your senior pastor before the announcements go out to anyone else. Ask him if it fits with the overall church agenda, and point out how each event supports the mission of the church.

> I forget this as well. A staff member just called us out on it and reminded us to create our calendars in collaboration. It helped so much. The rest of the year will be smooth sailing if it starts out like this.

Rally Around Your Church's Mission

If you were to ask your students right now to identify your church's mission, what would they say? And if they can quote it, do they know what it means to live it out? If your students can answer both of these questions, awesome job! If not, start now helping your students join in the mission of your church.

Integrate the church mission into your teaching, your language, and your small groups. Give your students concrete examples of how they can live out the mission, even as teenagers. Break the mission into manageable bites so they can easily understand it. Most adults treat teenagers as though they can't really uphold the church mission until they are an adult. No wonder many students believe this. Be the change agent that helps students to own their faith and adopt the mission of the church.

A high school girl went to her youth pastor one day burdened by the issue of poverty in the world. She really wanted to help people understand the crisis of poverty and its global effects, and to mobilize people of every age to get involved in ending it.

After much brainstorming, a poverty simulation evolved, which she called Journey to Awareness. Almost every student in the church went through a month of different experiences that included eating only rice for a whole day, sleeping on the floor, and wearing no shoes. The youth pastor followed up by integrating small group lessons and weekly teachings that dealt with God's heart for the poor.

This Journey to Awareness event became so powerful that church families couldn't help but notice the impact it was having on the teenagers. Eventually, the entire church adopted the Journey to Awareness into its calendar, and kicked it off by encouraging people to come to church on Sunday without any shoes on their feet. This all happened because one girl firmly believed in the mission of her church to make a difference in the world, and it changed the lives of so many.

Teenagers can have a great impact on the church. You get to be the one that shows them what your church's mission is and dream with them how they can make it a reality.

> This story is amazing, yet only possible if the youth pastor and senior pastor are partners. When they are teammates, their ministry is unleashed and the possibilities are endless.

Aligning a youth ministry with the church's overall mission can be challenging, but it is necessary and well worth it. Each of the action steps in this chapter—and in many cases, this entire book—are not "musts."

You have a vital role to initiate and develop a growing relationship with your church leaders—especially your senior pastor. You must work to build a unity that weathers many storms. Consider these words of encouragement as you lead this week:

And now, a word to you who are elders in the churches. I, too, am an elder and a witness to the sufferings of Christ. And I, too, will share in his glory when he is revealed to the whole world. As a fellow elder, I appeal to you: Care for the flock that God has entrusted to you. Watch over it willingly, not grudgingly—not for what you will get out of it, but because you are eager to serve God (1 Peter 5:1-2).

Here are some exercises for you (even better—for both you and your senior pastor) to process to help you effectively live in unity.

Church Family Profile

Assessment

If you are going through this book with your senior pastor, take 30 minutes this week to go through this activity on your own, and then meet with your senior pastor to discuss your thoughts. This assessment coincides with the senior pastor section of the book.

As discussed in the chapter, both you and your senior pastor are on the same mission of serving families, but you approach it from two different vantage points. In this activity you will take some time to think about the families of your church. Make sure to go through this activity together with your senior pastor so you can discuss your opinions and reasoning behind your thoughts and conclusions.

The goals for this exercise are as follows:

- Describe your view of the families in your church. Explore families' basic needs and areas that could use more attention by combining your observations with your senior pastor's.

- Design a plan for both you and your senior pastor to effectively develop families in your church. The plan should include steps to equip and encourage parents to become teenagers' primary faith influencers; build marriages that edify both spouses; and help both the parents and their teenagers to develop an owned faith.

Follow these steps to complete the Church Family Profile Assessment:

1. Assign percentages (rough estimates) to each of the items in the Church Family Profile on page 62. Work to come to a consensus on these, using information gleaned from your experiences.

2. If there are percentages you disagree on, discuss why you disagree and listen carefully to each other's experiences and involvement with families. It may be that several marriages are in crisis, but all the youth pastor is hearing from his students is that their parents just don't understand them. Several families might be putting on a good front, but the youth pastor has learned some of the behind-the-scenes problems from listening to their kids.

   Take some time to really examine any differences you have in your answers. Also, if any key areas tug at your heart, be sure to discuss them with each other.

3. If there is a demographic issue that is not listed on the Church Family Profile, add that to the chart and assign a percentage to it.

4. Discuss what major issues, patterns, and concerns arise after completing this profile. While both of you are on the same mission of ministering to families, you may be burdened in different ways, but bringing them to the forefront is important.

5. Lastly, select a few issues or areas of concern that you can team up on to help develop and equip the families in your church based on what you examined in this profile. Create action steps within these areas.

Examples...

- Cast the vision to parents during an event or dessert function describing their role and the church's role in ministering to teenagers.

   > Parents = Primary Faith Influencers

   > Church = Equipping parents to be Primary Faith Influencers, and developing teenagers who will own their faith

- Set up a parenting retreat or a few events that help equip parents of growing teenagers—especially in the areas of greatest need. Partner up as senior pastor and youth pastor to focus on youth culture, a home that cultivates spiritual growth, a Christ-centered family, and other relevant topics.

- Reach out to a specific need area, like single parenting, and spend one training session dealing with specific issues that this brings up.

- Take a month of small groups this year to focus on family dynamics/relationships and a need area from this profile (both for the parents and the youth).

Church Family Profile

Parents...
- ☐ Are strong disciples of Christ
- ☐ Know Christ, but following him is not a priority
- ☐ Are not Christ-followers

Families are...
- ☐ Two-Parent Homes
  - ☐ Married ☐ Not Married ☐ Blended (remarried)
- ☐ Single-Parent Homes
  - ☐ Divorced ☐ Widowed ☐ Never Married

Teenagers are...
- ☐ Owners of their faith
- ☐ Engaged with faith
- ☐ Apathetic
- ☐ Rejecting faith

Teenagers...
- ☐ Honor their parents
- ☐ Are in relationship with their parents
- ☐ Don't care about their parents

Dads are...
- ☐ Positive leaders
- ☐ Present
- ☐ Negative influencers
- ☐ Absent

Parents...
- ☐ Are aware of youth culture
- ☐ Think they're aware, but they're not
- ☐ Want to learn/ understand it
- ☐ Are unaware of youth culture

Moms are...
- ☐ Positive leaders
- ☐ Present
- ☐ Negative influencers
- ☐ Absent

Parents...
- ☐ Are primary faith influencers and desire partnership with the church
- ☐ Are primary faith influencers for their children but want no help
- ☐ Want to be significant faith influencers, but don't know how
- ☐ Arer elying completely on church to develop children's faith

Students are...
- ☐ Leading peers
- ☐ Growing in confidence
- ☐ Lacking self-esteem
- ☐ Just trying to survive

Families are...
- ☐ Strong, healthy, growing
- ☐ Surviving
- ☐ In crisis

Teenagers are...
- ☐ Trusting of adults and have healthy relationships with them
- ☐ Skeptical of adults, but open to relationship
- ☐ Avoiding or lying to adults

Parents are...
- ☐ Empowering their children
- ☐ Enabling their children (rescuing)
- ☐ Hovering/smothering their children
- ☐ Ignoring their children

Marriages are...
- ☐ Thriving
- ☐ Surviving
- ☐ In crisis
- ☐ Over/ Divorced

conclusion

{ youth pastor }

Throughout the process of writing this book, I've loved talking with youth pastors and senior pastors from around the country, and remembering my days as a youth pastor. But at the same time, a lot of sadness has come as I've hashed over old stories from my days in the church. Sadness, not because of what happened, but because of what didn't happen. Looking back, I realize now I did not truly see my relationship with any of my senior pastors the way I should have seen it. I never put the time and effort into building those relationships, and now, years down the road, I realize I am disconnected from the people I partnered with in ministry. Where I should have lasting friendships, I have nothing.

But it does not have to be this way. When you and your senior pastor are connected, you can truly serve and meet the needs of your congregation. Being united with your senior pastor helps you build momentum and excitement for the church staff and elder team. The kingdom difference is far greater as your impact spreads to adult ministries, and your senior pastor's impact spreads to students. Obstacles and challenges are all minimized. The future of your church becomes a place of excitement and dreaming, instead of a place of surviving and quitting. And at the end of the day, you'll be doing ministry—and life—with a trusted friend.

THE
disconnect

bridging the
senior pastor and **youth** pastor
gap

by
Doug Franklin

Every time your youth pastor leaves your office, you wonder what just happened. "Why aren't our youth headed the same direction as the rest of the church? Why aren't they connecting with our other ministries? Does my youth pastor really hear anything I say when we meet?"

Unfortunately, you aren't alone. When it works, the relationship between a senior pastor and youth pastor opens the door to dynamic ministry in the local church. But when that relationship is weak, damaged, or broken, it can create an environment that breeds frustration, dissension, and burnout.

And in far too many churches, that relationship *is* weak, damaged, or broken. Trust, respect, and sacrifice don't happen when we aren't on the same page.

Doug Franklin and the team at LeaderTreks tackle the challenge of restoring that relationship in *The Disconnect*, a unique resource that brings together senior pastors and youth pastors for honest dialogue on the tough task of working together. Doug writes directly to you as a senior pastor, offering his encouragement and wisdom.

In this book, you'll discover:
- How you and your youth pastor can more effectively communicate
- How core values can lead to greater respect
- Why ministry and money can't be separated
- How to align your expectations
- Why a shared mission is essential

If you're on the verge of firing your youth pastor because things just aren't working out, we encourage you to take time to read this book first. Perhaps the relationship can't be restored—but perhaps it can. A restored relationship will allow you to begin writing a new chapter in the life of your church.

If you and your youth pastor already communicate and work together well, this book will help you solidify that relationship. You can take something good and make it great.

Doug Franklin is the president of LeaderTreks, an innovative leadership development organization focusing on students and youth workers. He and his wife, Angie, live in West Chicago. Doug grew up in Illinois and is a graduate of Wheaton College. His passion is using experiential learning to help students and adults grow as leaders. Doug writes about leadership on his blog at dougfranklinonline.com.

The Disconnect
Bridging the Youth Pastor and Senior Pastor Gap

Copyright © 2011 Doug Franklin

group.com
simplyyouthministry.com

Credits
Author: Doug Franklin
Executive Developer: Nadim Najm
Chief Creative Officer: Joani Schultz
Editor: Michael Novelli
Copy Editors: Rob Cunningham and Janis Sampson
Cover Art and Production: Jeff A. Storm and Veronica Lucas
Production Manager: DeAnne Lear

Unless otherwise indicated, all Scripture quotations are taken from the *Holy Bible*, New Living Translation, copyright © 1996, 2004, 2007. Used by permission of Tyndale House Publishers, Inc., Carol Stream, Illinois 60188. All rights reserved.

Library of Congress Cataloging-in-Publication Data
Franklin, Doug, 1963-
  The disconnect : bridging the youth pastor and senior pastor gap / Doug Franklin.
    p. cm.
  ISBN 978-0-7644-6658-8 (pbk. : alk. paper)
  1. Church youth workers--Professional relationships. 2. Clergy--Professional relationships. I. Title.
  BV4447.F665 2011
  253'.2--dc22
                                2010052915

ISBN 978-0-7644-6658-8

10 9 8 7 6 5 4 3 2 1   20 19 18 17 16 15 14 13 12 11

Printed in the United States of America.

Dedication

This book is dedicated to my beautiful and creative wife,
Angie, who helped with this book more than you'll ever know.
Thank you, sweetheart.

—Doug

Contents

senior pastors

Start Here...

It was my first youth ministry job where I was the lead youth worker. The church was only a couple of years old and didn't yet have a senior pastor, but my youth ministry was thriving. Countless kids, churched and un-churched, were deepening or starting their relationship with Christ. I loved my job, but I knew I needed wisdom and mentoring. Needless to say, I was thrilled when the elders told me they were hiring a senior pastor. Even more exciting was that the new senior pastor was a former youth pastor and a well-known youth speaker. I envisioned a partnership in which he would not only lead me but also mentor me in ministry and in life. Together we would form the foundation of an amazing team, bringing people from all over our city through the doors of our church and into a relationship with Jesus. Our mission would move forward because we would be united.

When the senior pastor arrived, I was already busy planning a mission trip for my group. Having gotten approval from two dads who had been overseeing me, I presented my plan to the senior pastor, and to my delight he told me to "go for it." I continued my planning and even bought a flight ticket (with my senior pastor's approval) to set up the mission site.

Two weeks later I was asked to breakfast by a few elder members and the senior pastor. They didn't waste much time before they were drilling me about the mission trip and chastising me for making all the decisions without any authority. I tried to defend myself, telling them the senior pastor had told me to "go for it," but he claimed he had heard nothing about it. I was shocked and hurt, and for the first time realized the hard truth: My senior pastor and I were disconnected. Six months later I had resigned.

Looking back, I see many of the real problems that were hidden from me then: My senior pastor and I had not spent any real time getting to know each other on a personal or ministry level, we didn't understand each other's values, and we certainly were not on the same mission. Many of these things led to my resignation.

This disconnect saddens me, yet it is all too common. Many youth pastors end up leaving ministry because of unmet expectations regarding the relationship with their senior pastors. Is this the senior pastors' fault? Of course not, but they do need help in realizing the important role they play in keeping their youth pastor in ministry. Things don't go well in a youth ministry when the senior pastor and youth pastor are at odds, not talking, or holding judgments and grudges. The youth ministry, and the church as a whole, doesn't function at its best when the pastoral team is not unified. Trust, respect, and sacrifice don't happen when we aren't on the same page. The need is out there for senior pastors and youth pastors to be unified as they pursue a mission.

 Our churches *can* function with a staff that's not unified. But they *cannot* reach the potential God has dreamed for them.

As I sat down to write this book, I'll admit my time as a youth pastor steered much of my thinking about the subject matter. After all, it is my experiences, good and bad, which have shaped how I've served other youth workers for many years. While my experiences have proved effective in the advice I gave to most youth workers, I realized it could not be the only source material I worked from to write this book. To that end, much of what you read has come from not only my time as a youth worker but also from others around me. Through interviews with youth pastors and senior pastors and through multiple surveys, I gathered the needed information to write this book. Many of their stories are retold in my own words throughout these pages.

A couple things to know before you start…

1. **The comments in boxed text throughout the book mean something.** I sent out the finished chapters to youth pastors and senior pastors all around the country to get their specific thoughts regarding the content of this book. As you read, you'll notice this icon 🎤 along with comments or even personal stories relating to the material from many senior pastors who were once youth pastors. Much of the boxed text lends validity to my points, while others offer some pushback. I chose to include all these comments because the pages should display my heart behind this book. There are many opinions out there which deserve to be heard. No single piece of writing or individual conversation will solve all the problems you have in ministry. My hope and prayer is for you to find nuggets of truth contained in my writing or in the boxed text and apply them. If this book brings fruit to the relationship between you and your youth pastor, I have achieved my goal.

2. It takes two to tango. For every chapter written to youth pastors, there's a chapter on the same topic written to senior pastors. I tried to help youth pastors take steps to understand their senior pastors' point of view. And I did the same thing for senior pastors. Ideally, you will benefit the most from this book if both you and the youth pastor read it at the same time. Each exercise at the end of the chapter will be more helpful if you can debrief it together, but still beneficial if that's not possible.

3. You don't have to be at your wits' end to read this. I wrote this book because so many youth pastors came to me exasperated and ready to quit. If your relationship with your youth pastor is good, there is a lot of stuff in here that can help move it from good to great—from tweaking your communication style to gaining a common language and understanding of each other's core values. This is about developing unity in the church leadership so that the effect trickles down and builds a healthy culture in your entire church.

4. To all the women out there. This book is written using masculine pronouns in reference to the senior pastor and youth pastor. This was done just for the sake of readability. When I tried to write out things like "he or she" and "him or her" in every instance, the book became wordy and difficult to read. There are an equal number of women in leadership who are doing a phenomenal job, and I fully intend to honor that. I wrote in this language solely for readability.

chapter 1

{ senior pastor }

What I Heard You Say Was...

Using communication that counts

I t's funny how much of life and ministry boils down to communication. No wonder Jesus tirelessly communicated to people in different ways. He had a message to bring, but just saying it wasn't enough. Sometimes he taught in parables, giving illustrations that really "spoke their language." Sometimes he had casual conversation over dinner or preached from a mountainside. And sometimes he didn't use words at all, choosing instead to live out the very message he was preaching. Christ was a master of intentional communication.

Good communication is one of the hardest skills to hone, and often the priciest. Think about the conversations and counseling sessions you've had with couples whose marriages are struggling. If bad communication isn't the core of the problem, it's usually the fuel on the fire and may even destroy the marriage. Politicians spend millions of dollars to communicate the right message to the public. Marketing gurus make their living out of compelling and concise communication. And pastors, like you, have spent many tedious hours in crafting sermons to share God's truth. We all know the importance of good communication.

So, how is your communication with your youth pastor? How could it improve? If you two really worked at it, what would be the positive effects on the youth ministry, families, sermons, your staff, your church...and even your personal stress level?

In the surveying done to prepare for this book, youth pastors revealed that a lack of communication was the number one problem they were facing in relationships with their senior pastors. Other than entire church staff meetings and water-cooler conversations, youth pastors in general were not getting much communication from their senior pastors unless there were problems to address.

> My first senior pastor told me I was great to my face, while the whole time he talked behind my back about what he really thought. He never had the guts to come and tell me what he really thought and always made it someone else's complaint when he did, so as to shield himself from "being the bad guy." I read right through it, and it made me have no respect for him. He was my boss, but I knew that I didn't ever want to be mentored by the guy. He had no integrity as far as I was concerned. In fact, a lot of senior pastors operated this way. They have no guts, no courage to speak the truth in love and face the music of a response. It's one of the biggest reasons youth pastors don't respect their senior leaders.

Let's be honest. Youth pastors need help and support, and you could be the most influential person in their life. They need your wisdom, encouragement, and guidance. And believe it or not, most youth pastors really want *more* communication and input into their lives and ministry.

There's a "secret" that most youth workers tell their peers: "Bible college, internships, seminary [or whatever training it was] did not prepare me for this!" It's probably not something coming up in the interview process (or else no one would hire them), but it's a scary reality. When asked confidentially if they were prepared to serve in a church, most reply that they weren't. They were trained in the basics of youth ministry, but being trained to function in a church system is another story. After basic training, they fell into the deep end—creating budgets, managing volunteer staff, having hard conversations with church parents who are old enough to be his or her own parents and not to mention the whole slew of other "firsts" that they might be experiencing in their personal lives: new marriages, young families, first homes.

The solution? The help? Communication. There's no doubt a pastor's job is overwhelming already, but intentional communication from you could be the rope that pulls your youth pastor out of the deep end and empowers him to overcome obstacles, plant deep roots of trust in your church, and be a teammate that will be in it for the long haul with you.

Here are some ways you can use intentional communication to help your youth pastor.

Start With the "Why"

You can skip a lot of the trial and error process by giving the "why" behind your thinking. If it seems like your youth pastor is making the same mistakes, just in a different scenario, then he probably doesn't know the "why" behind your thinking.

For example: When a youth pastor goes out of town with students, calling parents to let them know their child has safely arrived is vital. However, just telling your youth pastor to call the parents or starting the phone tree is one thing. It's another thing entirely to tell them what goes through the parents' minds when they don't know if their child is safe and how that affects the youth ministry and keeps parents from respecting the youth pastor. Giving the "why" behind your instructions or expectations empowers the youth pastor to make great decisions even when the scenario changes.

> It would be helpful to communicate with your youth pastor how his ministry implementation and vision either fits with yours or is opposed to yours. It would be great to help unpack that for the youth pastor. Otherwise, the entrepreneurial youth pastor comes in and starts doing what he thinks is awesome and fits with all that he's learned about student culture, only to be slapped in the face when he is told that his ministry is not in line with the church's vision.

State the "why" behind church vision and mission as well. Communicate your heart, your plan, and the consequences up front, and watch your staff mobilize. If your staff is not moving forward with carrying the mission of the church, you can bet they don't really know the heart behind it. They must understand why it matters to you, the community, the families in the church, and God. Knowing the "why" behind your instructions keeps mistakes from being repeated, and it keeps inaction from taking place.

> The biggest mistake I made with a youth pastor was assuming that all of his training qualified him and made him an expert. I don't know why I assumed that—probably because I have so much on my plate that when we get a staff person who is an expert, I feel like I can just move that area of ministry off my plate. That was a huge mistake because it took away the mentoring desperately needed to navigate church culture.

Be Approachable

It's hard to deliver bad news. And youth ministry lends itself to some pretty bad news sometimes. Combine immature students with sugar and hormones, a handful of hovering parents, wacky games, and college-aged volunteers, and you're going to have bad news on occasion. You'll also have some life-changing kingdom moments, but they are probably coupled with hospital visits, broken relationships, or a run-in with a parent. The best thing you can do to help develop your youth pastor and protect the ministry is to be approachable.

Be the person your youth pastor comes to first with bad news because grace and gentle correction is waiting on your side of the desk. Not that there aren't

consequences, but there's a safety and freedom in breaking bad news to you. You can help to become this person in your youth pastor's life by regularly initiating communication. Stop by his office. Sit down for no other reason than to lend a listening ear. Approaching your youth pastor in his setting demonstrates that you care and that what he is doing is meaningful.

No Communication = Negative Assumptions

When interactions are down, there's a lot of room for insecurities and doubts to rise. People tend to assume the worst in the midst of silence. They become unsure of where they stand. Thoughts like "He doesn't really care about my ministry" or "This is awesome—I don't have to check in with him" or "My senior pastor never encourages me" filter into the thinking. When you don't regularly check in or interact with your youth pastor, he will most likely begin to assume there's a problem. The funny thing is we often don't check in with the ministry leaders that are doing really well because they don't need as much help. But that can actually hurt the situation more than help it.

> I remember the first church I worked in. After I began to preach, people started to ask if I could preach more often. They said that they enjoyed listening to me. They even approached the senior pastor about this. I could tell that this hurt and threatened him. But we never talked about it. In fact, I could tell that our relationship changed after that. I was just using my gifts, the gifts that God had given me, but they directly challenged the role that the senior pastor was supposed to be in. But we never talked about that, and being a brash young whippersnapper, I let it go to my head and began to think that I could do the senior pastor's job better than he could. If he would have told me how that made him feel or where he was at with my preaching gifts, I think I would have felt compassionate toward him and supported him better.

Listen Deeply

Listening deeply to your youth pastor can begin to pave the road that gives you permission to speak truth into his life. Listen deeply by peeling back the layers

of his comments and helping him get to the heart of the issue. A comment like "This Wednesday night wasn't that great because hardly any kids showed up" is an opener for you to ask questions, see what's really bothering your youth pastor (is his focus off, are his expectations wrong, or is it spring break?), and help him plan strategically for the future. A comment like "The retreat was awesome" is an opener for you to peel back the layers and talk about how your youth pastor measures success and what's important to him. Listening deeply (and building trust) will let you get to the heart of your youth pastor and allow opportunities for impromptu mentoring and training.

Gain a Platform

Youth pastors will respect and listen to their senior pastors when they have to (I hope so, anyway). But to really gain a place of influence in their lives, you need to earn it. Have you ever offered advice to your youth pastor and felt like he just emptily nodded back? It probably means you have your work cut out for you. You can pull the boss card, and there are probably times that you should, but how much more meaningful is your communication if the youth pastor seeks it out, heeds the advice, and eagerly follows? If you have that kind of relationship already, be grateful and continue to cultivate it. If you don't, pursue him, be consistent, and be a leader worth following.

Get a Large Perspective of Your Influence

If your youth pastor is in his first years of ministry, your communication is vital not only for his current season but also for his ministry 25 years from now. In his first years, he will form some deep patterns, beliefs, and habits of ministry. You have a golden opportunity to impact the kingdom in a huge way by helping him gain a strong start. Your influence now will make a difference in your youth pastor's influence 25 years from now.

It's a lot easier to hear stuff from someone who you know cares about you, who has taken an interest in you as a person, and who seems genuinely interested in your growth as a minister. Hanging out or doing something fun is an awesome way to facilitate communication. When I was given the task of supervising a youth pastor, we played golf, hung out for lunch, and developed a relationship. Out of that, it's much easier to talk about tough stuff and much easier for your youth pastor to share his struggles with you and to tell you what's on his heart.

Most youth pastors feel overwhelmed and under prepared for their jobs. Your ability to communicate with your youth pastor could give you a voice in his life that trains him for some incredible kingdom impact. Your influence now has great implications later, and that journey begins with initiating regular communication.

Intentional Communication

Assessment

The following is an assessment to help determine how intentional your communication is with your youth pastor. While this assessment will be helpful, ultimately you know best what you are doing well and what needs to improve in the communication that you share.

If you are going through this book with your youth pastor, take 30 minutes this week to go through this activity on your own, and then meet with your youth pastor to discuss your thoughts. This assessment coincides with the youth pastor section of the book.

1. Are your meetings (aside from entire church staff meetings) spontaneous or planned?
   a. Always spontaneous
   b. Half and half
   c. Usually planned

2. What is your attitude going into a meeting with your youth pastor?
   a. I avoid it.
   b. I tolerate it.
   c. I have a positive attitude about it.

3. How well does your youth pastor know your ministry?
   a. He knows the ministry numbers.
   b. He knows the basic schedule of events.
   c. He knows the "why" behind the ministry and its greatest needs.

4. How well do you understand the pressures your youth pastor is facing?
   a. I think I know what they are, but I'm not certain.
   b. I am aware of the pressures he's facing.
   c. I offer support and pray for him as he faces these pressures.

5. How often do you feel that your youth pastor just doesn't get your approach to ministry?
   a. Very often. He just doesn't understand me or the church's ministry.
   b. He sometimes gets it, but has too many other concerns.
   c. He asks good questions and tries hard to understand the church's ministry and me.

6. How well have you communicated the purpose behind your church's ministry programming?
   a. I give a report on what activities we are doing every year.
   b. I've laid out the church's ministry plan and a reason for each part of it.
   c. I regularly meet and share about why we are doing each of our programs, their impact and challenges.

7. How well do you know your youth pastor?
   a. I know a little about him and his approach to ministry.
   b. I know him on a personal level, and I'm beginning to understand what motivates him.
   c. I know him well, and his heart and dreams for ministry.

8. How much evaluation do you provide for your youth pastor?
   a. We evaluate once a year, and when issues arise.
   b. A few times a year, especially after an event.
   c. We regularly discuss his overall performance .

9. Do you know what "a job well done" looks like to your youth pastor?
   a. I am not sure what he considers "a job well done."
   b. I have an idea, but I had to learn it the hard way—through trial and error.
   c. I know what my youth pastor expects from me and what he considers a good job.

10. When my youth pastor and I meet, we communicate about
    a. Problems and concerns mostly.
    b. Logistics/calendar and problems.
    c. Our ministries' progress and needs, and personal life issues.

Add up your scores below.

A_____ B_____ C_____

Based on your scores, take a look at what category your communication fits into, and come up with an action plan that you can initiate this week to help make your communication more intentional.

A's = 2 or more and C's = 2 or less

If you had more than 2 A's and less than 2 C's, your communication with your youth pastor is not very intentional. It's probably lacking in both quality and quantity and could have some potential bitterness and judgments mixed up with it. This type of communication tends to lead toward negative assumptions by both parties and a natural division. Although you may be able to function together, you are not reaching the full potential of what a unified team in ministry can reach. Consider taking the following steps: First, begin praying specifically for your youth pastor daily. This can often change some of our own attitudes and understanding of someone. Second, ask for a time when you and your youth pastor can meet and you can talk over the overall strategic plan of the church with him and how the youth ministry fits into it. Make sure to include the "why" behind each point of it and cast the vision for him (don't forget to include your heart behind it). This will take time, and possibly several attempts, but it could open the door to a new type of communication and a new platform for your relationship.

Action Step:

A's = 1 or more and C's = 3 or less

If you had 1 or more A's and less than 4 C's, your communication with your youth pastor is somewhat regular but not as intentional as it could be. You have a foundation built on communication, but interactions are more transactional than they are intentional. Your communication has some necessary logistic and calendar focus but not much more than that. Start asking your youth pastor for the "why" or purpose behind the logistics and calendar that he brings up, practice listening deeply for clues into what is burdening him in the ministry, and offer encouragement for when he's propelling the church's mission forward. Use small moments and casual interactions to build unity and trust with your youth pastor by listening deeply, identifying the root of any obstacles or problems, and coaching

your youth pastor through it. This may transform your relationship into a chance to mentor or guide your youth pastor in his future ministry potential.

Warning: Check your heart! Are you playing church office politics, or do you really care about your youth pastor?

Action Step:

A's = 0 and C's = 4 or more

If you had no A's and more than 4 C's, your communication has a strong foundation and is pretty intentional. Continue the road you are on, and grow your relationship by going out of the way to serve and support your youth pastor. Move into the level of "soul care" and be a ministry mentor. Offer a good mix of respect and encouragement. This will most likely lead to reciprocation and an even stronger, healthier relationship. Consider hanging out with your youth pastor in a social setting, such as at a ball game.

Action Step:

chapter 2

{ senior pastor }

Aretha Franklin Said It Best...

How core values can lead to respect

Most youth pastors I know hate fundraising, myself included. Pizza sales, yard work, and car washes don't get too many people excited. Fundraising is a necessary evil for most youth pastors though. If you plan on doing any kind of mission trip or weekend retreat, at some point your students will have to raise the funds. This was the case when, in my second year as the youth pastor, I found myself walking into my senior pastor's office with questions about fundraising for the summer mission trip. To my complete surprise, my current senior pastor was thrilled to be involved in the process of helping the students raise funds. He was passionate about the students going on a mission trip and wanted to do everything he could to help, including getting the entire church on board.

He came up with the best idea I have to this day ever seen: a churchwide auction. But instead of getting products from local stores or restaurant coupons, he had three women call everyone in the church, asking them to auction off their time or talents. Guitar professors donated ten private lessons, couples offered a dinner night at their house, one woman gave homemade specially designed cakes, and a family donated their lake house for a week. As the three women kept calling people throughout the church and explaining the mission trip auction night, more donations kept coming in. The senior pastor also lined up two dads to help me plan all the logistics of the night so I wouldn't be overwhelmed. It was amazing.

When the night finally arrived, everyone was excited. The two dads stood by the entry door, assigning auction numbers to each person or family as they walked in. Our students, led by our "Italian Chef" mother/daughter combo, cooked and served the most amazing spaghetti dinner. The senior pastor had also asked the church loud-mouth to be the auctioneer, and he performed flawlessly. The whole night was filled with laughter and conversation. As I stood in the back of the room, I watched an entire church embrace the youth group's vision—it brought me to tears. The event raised over $12,000, which easily covered every student and my adult staff for the mission trip. The auction had promoted our student ministry, deepened relationships in the church, and created a night of lasting fun. In fact, every year people asked me when the auction would be and told me their new ideas for donations. And all of this was possible because my senior pastor valued our youth ministry. At his core he valued the students, believing they could make a huge difference—not only in the church but in the world as well.

Everyone has core values. Core values are simply a set of internal principles hard wired into your DNA, acting like a compass. They guide our behavior, affect our attitude, and influence our decisions on a daily basis. These rules, or personal guides, are extremely important to an individual. Violating someone's core values can strike

a nerve, but respecting and encouraging them can be a catalyst for success, both in an individual's performance and in team unity.

As the senior pastor in your church, your core values are likely imbedded into the expectations and culture of the church—not necessarily because you impose them on people, but because you are the key influencer of the church. People are watching you and using your actions to set a standard of expectations. If you are never late to work, your staff will feel pressure if they are late. If you come late often, your staff will probably start streaming in late as well. The style you use to run meetings will probably be adopted by others when they run meetings. In many ways, you are the standard bearer, with your core values permeating the culture.

This is not a bad thing. In fact, it's a great opportunity for you as a leader. My senior pastor's value for student service created unity and excitement throughout our whole church. As the senior pastor of your church, you have been given a small part of God's kingdom to build and guide. The Maker of the universe has entrusted you with a part of his precious plan. The downside is that without other people living out their core values in the church, the culture is likely to become imbalanced.

Each person can only have a handful of core values. There are definitely more things we value—and we should if we are following God's Word—but there are only a handful of principles that make up your gut reactions and natural inclinations. Only a few things are woven so deeply into your core that it is almost impossible to make a decision that violates those values. One of your most powerful tools as a leader is the ability to create space and freedom for your staff members to excel in their own core values. This will create a strong and balanced church that can weather many storms.

Below are examples of three members of a church staff. Take a look at the core values of each individual and how they differ.

Note: Values often coincide and interchange with their wiring or passions.

Person A	Person B	Person C
Legacy	Adventure	Helping/Serving Others
Teaching	Teamwork/Cooperation	Understanding
Influencing Others	Personal Freedom	Healing/Wholeness
Growth/Improvement	Prayer	Peace/Tranquility
Commitment	Knowledge/Learning	Fairness/Justice

If all three of these staff members lived out their own core values in their jobs and also respected and encouraged each other's core values, this would be a dynamic leadership team. But the easiest thing to do when we're tired, insecure, or under stress is to revert back to our natural inclinations, making our own values king. All of us would probably tip our hats to each value on the list and acknowledge its significance, but our actions would fall in line with our own core values.

Go back and take a look at each of the staff members listed, and imagine what a church would be like if it operated primarily by only one person's core values. Person A would have a very strategic church but would have a lot of turnover and would risk running over some people. Person B would have a community-driven church that might lack direction or growth. Person C would have a church focused on renewal and healing but would probably face burnout down the road. Without the entire team's core values guiding decisions, these individual churches would not be healthy.

As the primary leader in your church, you have the ability to not only embrace the core of your team members but also make space for their values and empower them to respect and encourage each other's values.

Take a look at these signifiers that let you know when team members are feeling like they are living out their own values on the job. See if these statements describe your staff members—especially your youth pastor:

- They seem satisfied, not worn out.

- They're responsible and trustworthy; they don't drop balls or disappoint.

- They're connected to the overall mission and the team.

- They take appropriate risks because they are risking from a confident and fulfilled mind-set.

- They display and encourage positive attitudes.

Staff members who don't feel free to live out their core values on the job will probably spend a lot more time focusing on how to align their thoughts, ideas, and performance to your core values. They are less likely to participate in offering ideas, take on new responsibilities, and take ministry risks. They are more focused on pleasing you—maybe even more than pleasing God—than on living out their own strengths to the best of their abilities.

Here are some signifiers to let you know when team members feel their values are being violated or they are unable to live them out on the job:

- They focus too much on small problems or on one issue.

- They become overly sensitive or touchy. They lack a sense of humor.

- They overreacts to situations and become judgmental.

- They seem to be pushing their own agenda or viewpoint much of the time.

- They act frustrated with not being heard or give off the impression that they are outsiders.

If your youth pastor (or any staff member) is showing signs that his values are being violated, it's not necessarily your fault. But you do have the ability to change the situation because of your influence and leadership. If all of your staff members have the ability to live out their core values, knowing you have their back, you'll be an unstoppable force!

Depending on the team dynamic and leadership culture of your church, try some of the following action steps to create space for each staff member to live out hisr core values, while still maintaining boundaries and the mission of the church.

Change Up Your Meetings

When it comes to staff meetings, many follow the same format: a quick devotional, announcements of new decisions and events, an idea from the latest book you're reading, and a few minutes of personal updates and prayer requests.

How we run meetings often reflects our own values. When meetings take on the same format each time, the same people tend to do all the talking. The same people present problems, and the same people present solutions. Even internally, we can end up being frustrated by the same people after every meeting, yet thrilled with another person. How we run meetings often reflects our own values. Each time a meeting is run the same way (regardless of content), these attitudes and emotions will grow stronger.

Change up your meetings by focusing on the team, and encourage people to communicate in various ways.

Have Team Reports: Have each person give a team report or a "state of the union" for his area, but not based on the typical criteria. Have him give it based on a list of questions you provide, such as

- Why do I serve at this church?

- Describe two moments when you saw God really alive and active in your area?

- What was a time you were most satisfied in your role over the past month?

- How do you see your area of responsibility living out the mission of the church?

- What part of your role are you most excited about?

I *love* these questions and the meeting-change idea—it speaks in an arena where many senior pastors are comfortable enough to allow for change.

Have one meeting a month that another staff member leads: Whenever people face a change or a break in routine, they begin to align their actions and attitudes based on their true core values, not on a routine of reactions from the past. By having another individual run the meeting, it shows your staff members you care about giving them freedom and the ability to live out their core values.

Hang Out With Your Youth Pastor, but Leave Work at Church

Professional ministry can be daunting and leave us feeling overwhelmed. This usually leads to interactions based on ministry problems or empty emotions. It's easy to stop by the youth pastor's office to ask a quick question about a church family or schedule. And occasionally we have to stop by to confront a problem or get all the facts. These interactions are necessary, but they won't do much for creating team unity or building a sense of empowerment.

Sometimes making space for your youth pastor to live out his values on the job means getting to know how he lives them out off the job. Make some time to hang out with your youth pastor, without any work agenda. Go to a local game, invite his family to join your family for movie night, or go out for dinner as couples. This will grow your youth pastor's confidence in you and empower him to bring his core values to work. When your youth pastor feels like you are interested in him outside of work, he will most likely begin to translate that into work as well. If he can live authentically on neutral ground with you, he will feel more comfortable to live authentically on church ground.

Being a friend to your youth pastor doesn't mean you can't lead him. He still needs to hear evaluation, encouragement, and vision from you. But he will hear it more clearly if you're in relationship with him.

I thought immediately of the first senior pastor I served with. He was the kind of senior pastor who was easy to talk to. Although he wasn't overflowing with pulpit skills, he would often take me out to a local diner for a fish and chips lunch, and we'd shoot the breeze about marriage, finances, or handling criticism from church members. He and his wife sometimes stopped by our apartment to drop off an extra loaf of bread they'd baked or apples they'd picked. So when I preached my very first sermon, I was actually looking forward to his critique. I figured that I wouldn't pick up great pointers on delivery from him, but I also knew that he had wise insights into life and truth. Actually, some of his evaluation wasn't easy to hear, but I knew it was true. And I still wanted to hear it because I knew that he cared for me. Twenty years later, my wife and I still reminisce about how great it was to serve under someone who was so "for" us.

Have an Honest Conversation About Core Values

Talking openly and honestly about why you do the things you do and your core passions in ministry will always help. Get to know what your youth pastor's core values are and why they are so ingrained in him.

The profile at the end of this chapter will help you and your youth pastor put a name and definition to your core values. The importance of core values is that when we live by them, we tend to be at our best. We fire on all cylinders. But when they are not honored, we tend to be at our worst. Our life and ministry becomes off balance.

Both you and your youth pastor will go through the following activity to help identify both of your core values and make space for them at work.

Discovering Core Values

Profile

On pages 28-29, you will find a list of 81 different core values. This list will serve as the basis for helping you discover your core values. As you glance down the page, you may decide that in some way or another you actually value every item on the list. While that may be true, know that the point of the exercise is to unearth the few values that are absolutely essential to who you are and how you were created. This will be a challenge, as true self-discovery always is. But if you take this exercise seriously, it will help you understand more concretely your mode of operation.

If you are going through this book with your youth pastor, take 30 minutes this week to go through this activity on your own, and then meet with your youth pastor to discuss your thoughts. This profile coincides with the youth pastor section of the book.

IMPORTANT! Complete each step before moving on to the next one.

1. As you read each core value listed at the end of this chapter, decide whether you would consider it **somewhat important** in your day-to-day life or **important**. If you consider it to be **somewhat important**, draw a line through the word, crossing it out. Go through the whole list using this approach. Do not give too much thought to your choices, go with your first reaction.

2. Once you've completed this first step, go back through the list once again, only reading the words that are **not** crossed out. As you read each core value listed, decide in your head whether you would consider it **important** in your day-to-day life or **very important**. If you consider it to be **important**, draw a line through the word, crossing it out. Go through the whole list using this approach.

3. Once you've completed this second step, go back through the list once again, only reading the words that are not crossed out. As you read each core value listed, decide whether you would consider it **very important** in your day-to-day life or **extremely important**. If you consider it to be **very important**, draw a line through the word, crossing it out. Go through the whole list using this approach.

4. Repeat this whole process until you have narrowed the list down to no more than three to five core values that are **extremely important** to you.

Now that you've completed the search for your core values, it's time to ask yourself some key questions regarding these values and how they play into your life.

Where did your core values come from?

Core values tend to originate from three main sources: influential people, meaningful Scripture verses, and significant life experiences. Take some time to examine each of the core values you've discovered, and ask yourself where its existence stems from in your life. Knowing the origin helps you and others understand the core value's presence in your life.

Why do each of these values remain important to you?

Knowing where your values come from is not enough; it's imperative to also understand why these values are extremely significant in your life today. Spend a few moments and go through each value, taking time to think about why the value is remains important in your life today.

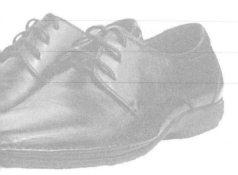

How do my core values affect my church?

This is a very significant question and is extremely pertinent to the discussion with your youth pastor. Your core values deeply affect the way you run your ministry and the way you perceive value within the ministry. Go through your core values and write down how you see them affecting the church you lead.

What are your youth pastor's core values?

After working alongside your youth pastor for weeks, months, and years, it may seem abundantly clear to you the core values present in his life. Write down the values you think are central to your youth pastor and how you see these values lived out on a regular basis.

How can you help?

In ministry, as in life, respecting another person's core values is key to maintaining an intentional relationship. Think of ways that you can personally show significance to your youth pastor through his core values and maybe even raise the level to which you value those qualities.

Discipleship	Mentoring	Community	Evangelism
Influencing Others	Safety/Security	Knowledge/ Learning	Personal Freedom
Cooperation/ Teamwork	Variety	Understanding	Hard Work
Tolerance	Risk Taking	Winning	Faith
Family	Hope	Initiative	People
Productivity	Achievement	Control	Pioneering
Beauty	Balance	Unity	Change
Authenticity	Consistency/ Dependability	Decency	Gratitude
Fun	Fulfillment	Friendships/ Relationships	Experiences
Empowerment	Creativity	Concern for Individuals	Simplicity
Success	Competence	Truth	Transformation

Love	Challenge	Excellence/Quality	Generosity
Forgiveness	Potential	Compassion/Mercy	Opportunity
Self-Renewal	Intimacy	Significance	Innovation
Impact	Trust	Time/Freedom	Purity
Responsibility	Respect	Purpose	Integrity
Honesty	Power	Prayer	Character
Sensitivity	Self-Worth	Duty	Perseverance
Loyalty	Courage	Prestige/Reputation	Money/Wealth
Joy	Kindness	Perfection	Humility
Shepherding			

chapter 3

{ senior pastor }

Ministry Is Where the Money Is...

If that were true, we wouldn't have this chapter

In churches and ministries across the country, money is a tough subject, but it's a really important one to address. After all, Jesus talks about money more than he talks about heaven, hell, or any other sin.[1] Maybe people in ministry struggle talking about money because we have developed so many misconceptions about money within ministry. We have taken Paul's words to Timothy about the evil of greed and applied it straight to money itself (1 Timothy 6:10). But money itself is not evil. There are some healthy ways we should treat and handle it, yet there are also some unhealthy realities existing in our churches, solely because we are broken people.

Money can bring about great things in ministry when used correctly, and it can show real value to people as well, but it can also send the wrong messages, causing wrong beliefs about money to emerge. There are several myths many people in ministry often believe:

- I should be content, no matter what.

- It's all part of sacrifice.

- It's wrong for me to ask for more pay.

- I don't have a retirement or college plan for my kids, but there are people starving in the world, so I should be happy.

There is some truth found in these beliefs, but they are not entirely true, and they often keep us from confronting some fundamental problems in our church system. Worse yet, they become the fertilizer for dysfunction, judgment, self-righteousness, and destructive behavior. Whether we like it or not, what we make is often on our minds. Many youth workers also look at what other staff and their senior pastors are making. Internally, they begin asking questions like "Do they deserve it?" or "Why don't I get paid as much?" or "Is this really what other pastors live on?" or "Why does my senior pastor get to live in that house?"

Financial pressure mixed with these kind of internal questions can lead a person down the path of "I deserve." Pretty soon, instead of looking at ministry through the vision and calling we began with, we look at it through what "I deserve" rather than what I can give. And any opportunity (which is a lot) that falls outside of the "I deserves" gets missed. Staff members become divided in this situation, and without unity, there isn't much that can get done.

One youth pastor interviewed for this book described in vivid detail how these questions appeared in his own life. Early on in ministry he took a job as high school youth pastor at a church, accepting the first salary offered—but then didn't receive

1. Piper, John. *The Appearance of the Unwasted Life, Part 1.* What Does this Life Look Like? Regional Conference, San Luis Obispo. March 29, 2008. desiringgod.org/resource-library/resources/the-appearance-of-the-unwasted-life-part-1

any compensation or increase for five years. Looking back, it appeared as though the church had wanted to squeeze as much out of its staff with as little pay as possible. They low-balled his salary, knowing how eager the recent college grad was to gain experience in ministry. Over the next five years, this youth pastor took on even more responsibility. He was soon overseeing the middle school, high school, and college ministries, as well as teaching every few Sundays. Eventually, he became a father and small children added to his expenses. The financial pressures were getting heavy and the load of responsibilities was growing—yet still the church leadership did not increase his salary.

The youth pastor went back and forth between thinking that the sacrifice he was making was meaningful in the kingdom and feeling completely devalued by the church. Mentally, he felt less and less on the mission of the church because it seemed like the church didn't care about him.

Eventually an elder of the church decided to meet with each of the staff members individually. The elder took the youth pastor out to lunch and just began asking basic questions about his family and how ministry was going. When the elder started hearing about the pressures in the family (marriage pressures because he and his wife couldn't really go out and spend alone time, since paying for a babysitter was out of the question, and so on) he started asking about finances. When the elder heard that no increase of salary had been given in five years, he was appalled. He immediately went back and made the other elders aware of it. The elder board soon voted on a pay-raise for the youth pastor and also examined the salaries of other staff members. Ultimately, this elder became an advocate for the youth pastor. He took the time to understand the pressures the youth pastor was facing, and he stood up for him.

Many youth pastors feel like they are viewed as big kids rather than the parents, employees, professionals, and the leaders that they are. Many youth pastors come right out of college and into ministry. Without job market experience or sophistication, they are suddenly handed a great responsibility. They go from living in a dorm to paying their own bills, managing budgets, leading a staff, creating programs, and participating in church leadership meetings. They often jumped into ministry with little to no experience and are trying to learn as they go. Many of them have young families and wonder how on earth they are going to meet the needs of their spouses, children, church, and students.

Too often, youth pastors feel they can't stand up for themselves when it comes to money issues. They don't feel they can approach elder boards directly, as that may be perceived as trying to circumvent you as their boss. They also may feel like their job is in jeopardy if they bring up a pay raise to you. Your youth pastor may be

thinking about leaving because he interprets his low salary as devaluing. The elder in the story above was a lifesaver for the youth pastor. Burnout, debt problems, family dissension, and many other issues were possibly avoided because the elder advocated for the youth pastor. The elder stood against the storm and wouldn't let the youth pastor get trampled. He infused new life into the youth pastor, giving him value, appreciation, and respect.

This does not mean that you should give your youth pastor a raise right now! Many of you are probably thinking that you haven't even gotten a raise, or times are tough and the church does not have the resources available. That's OK, but if the story I shared is happening in your church, communication is needed. You should be aware of your youth pastor's well-being, including how he is doing financially. If communication about salary isn't been offered on a regular basis, your youth pastor may be feeling devalued in his current role. Lack of communication often leads to negative assumptions. And that road can lead to disunity and possibly losing a staff member.

To help your youth pastor from going to down the path of "I deserve," here are a few things you can do to show understanding and value to him.

Seek to Understand Your Youth Pastor's Needs and Pressures

There are pressures weighing on your youth pastor that you may not even know. Those pressures aren't necessarily your problem, but if you understood them, your youth pastor would feel valued and respected—two feelings many people seek from the size of their paychecks. It will help your youth pastor overcome judgment, lack of mercy, and even gossip. Your youth pastor needs to feel understood. You may have already walked in his shoes, but this is the first time for him. Take the time to walk beside him for a little while and offer some extra value.

At the end of this chapter are a series of questions that you and your youth pastor can go through together to help bring understanding about finances.

Be Careful Not to Be a Source of Pressure

Many churches operate—although it's unspoken—on the idea of squeezing as much out of their staff as possible, at as little pay as possible. This should not be. Use salary to give freedom, show value, and offer respect. Imagine if you were the church in your town that paid their people more than the national median for no other reason than to empower them to lead others in the kingdom. This type of thinking would offer a sense of freedom and dreaming that financially pressed

people don't often hold. This type of thinking could create a culture of teamwork and sacrifice instead of the disunity and self-righteousness of the "I deserve" mentality.

 If you cannot pay the youth pastor what you want to pay him because of overall financial issues, have an open dialogue with him about it. Don't ignore it, hoping he won't notice or bring it up. Tell him the situation the church is in and how the elder board or finance team is attacking the problem. But don't promise what you are not sure you cannot deliver.

Offer Help With Financial Planning

If your church already offers financial planning classes, strongly encourage your youth pastor to participate. These classes offer great insight into how to steward your money from a biblical view. If your church doesn't offer a class, consider buying financial coaching material for your youth pastor, or even entire church staff, to go through.[2] These products may cost a bit up front, but are worth it in the long run. Having a staff that views finances from a godly perspective is always a benefit for the entire church.

Become an Advocate

Money isn't the only way you can be an advocate, but it's a start. You can help your youth pastor by singing his praises to the elders, taking him before the board and into the budget meetings, and asking for more on his behalf because you understand his financial situation and pressures. One of the most powerful things you can do is become an advocate for your youth pastor. Advocating his hard work. Advocating his salary. Advocating his need for an assistant or time off or whatever. After you understand where your youth pastor is coming from, become his advocate.

You can also become an advocate by applauding the youth pastor's hard work and offering good "gossip" whenever possible. It won't be a surprise when people support the youth ministry through all sorts of avenues (time, resources, places, and so on) when you take every opportunity to be an advocate for it.

---

2. Both Crown Financial Ministries and Dave Ramsey offer great financial education materials.

Use a Different Kind of Economy

In the corporate world, bonuses go a long way. They offer incentive and reward for sacrifice and hard work. In the ministry world, they are not always an option. The nice thing is, the ministry world can operate in a different kind of economy—a whole community of people who are willing to help, loan, and donate if they know there's a need. The key words here are "if they know there's a need." One way to encourage your staff is to pass on some of the offers that you get as the senior pastor. If someone has offered you a lake house for a weekend getaway, see if they would be willing to loan another weekend for the youth pastor. If you often receive gift cards for restaurants, pass a few on to the youth pastor. The amount of resources in the congregation can be staggering. And the generosity can be surprising. For many in your congregation, the chance to serve is a blessing for them. See if you can pass on any opportunities or benefits to the youth pastor as he demonstrates hard work and sacrifice.

> Conversation with your youth pastor will help you understand how to speak his love language. Speak it often. Better yet, make sure the church communicates to his spouse in a way that she knows he and his family are valued.

Oftentimes the financial issues a person is having are an indicator of other problems and pressures. It's not always as cut-and-dry as giving a raise or offering a bonus. The end goal is to understand and to advocate—not just for money, but also for support. Your youth pastor may have formed false ideas and judgments about money and budgets in the church. A youth pastor that feels understood and supported will be much more likely to dismiss falsehoods and reciprocate your support. Ultimately, these conversations build a stronger team and a more complete sense of unity. Debunking falsehoods leaves no room for grumbling, complaining, or impure motives.

Money Perceptions

Assessment

If you are going through this book with your youth pastor, take 30 minutes this week to go through this activity on your own, and then meet with your youth pastor to discuss your thoughts. This assessment coincides with the youth pastor section of the book.

Take some time and respond to the following questions.

How much stress does money or things related to money put on you?

1	2	3	4	5	6	7	8	9	10

None   It's overwhelming

How much stress does money or things related to money put on your family relationships?

1	2	3	4	5	6	7	8	9	10

None   It's overwhelming

How well do you feel like you are managing your personal finances?

1	2	3	4	5	6	7	8	9	10

Not very well   Very well

Is your attitude positive or negative toward your church when it comes to matters of money?

1	2	3	4	5	6	7	8	9	10

Negative   Positive

What specific challenges are you facing in your personal life financially?

In what ways are you and the church leadership praying about the financial pressures of the church?

How easy or difficult is tithing for you? Why?

What is the lack of money keeping you from doing in your ministry? Be specific.

How often do you make decisions based on large donor provisions versus God's provision?

Do you feel like you understand the financial situation of your youth pastor, both personally and in the youth ministry?

Based on your answers, what warning signs or areas do you see that need to change (such as attitude, tithing, stewardship, poor decision making)? Take a minute to write down why that area is a problem for you, and spend some time confessing it.

Now take a minute to write down some growth steps on how you plan to change this problem area in your life starting this week.

Example: I'm not going to give in to the pressure of making decisions based on donors. Every money decision I make this week, I will make in light of God's provision over donor provision. I will also work to address that thinking to our staff during staff meeting this week.

chapter 4

{ senior pastor }

I Wanted a Cadillac, but I Got a Chevy...

Aligning Your Expectations

The time we are most clear and precise about job expectations with our youth pastors is during and shortly after the hiring process. We spend time detailing and discussing their job description, describing in length their responsibilities, church policies, and church culture. This is a necessary and helpful process. But, most likely, things have changed since then: A staff member is gone, the church has taken on new initiatives, or maybe you discovered your youth pastor has some skills you never even knew about. And even more likely, your youth pastor heard or assumed something different than you meant.

As time passes, the expectations you and the church set can grow foggy or even get crowded out of your youth pastor's mind. Most youth pastors agree that college, seminary, and internships never prepared them for their job in youth ministry. It can also be translated as "I didn't expect this" or "I had no idea," when it comes to their job. No matter how much training and talking went on, being in the thick of ministry brings them to a whole new perspective. The expectations that were clear in the beginning may become unclear and start leading toward assumptions.

While a lack of clarity can bring some people energy as they create their own approaches to ministry, they might be moving in a direction that doesn't align with your church's vision and values. Whether the expectations have changed or were never laid out fully in the beginning, being unclear about current expectations only breeds disaster.

One senior pastor, Steve, communicated the expectation that the parents should be in the loop of *everything* that was happening in the youth ministry. Tim, the youth pastor, saw an annual parent meeting to discuss the calendar as a way to accomplish that. Unfortunately, he also felt that the parent meeting was enough to completely meet that expectation. He felt that ongoing communication with parents wasn't important—it was only repetitive.

Eventually, Tim got in the habit of leaving voice mails in his inbox until it was too full to accept any more. Parents grew furious at their inability to reach or ask questions of him. Quickly, the frustration of unhappy parents was heard loudly by Steve.

Steve called Tim into his office, furious that 27 voice mails had not been answered. What could Tim have possibly been thinking? Tim, on the other hand, was surprised by Steve's response and couldn't believe he was supposed to answer 27 voice mails of parents who were "too lazy" to look at the calendar and information they received in the parent meeting. After all, Tim put a lot into that meeting.

Expectations were definitely missed that day, even though both parties thought they were clearly communicated and clearly understood. It's hard to align your

expectations with someone else's expectations. Lack of clarity and regular communication leaves room for frustration and a breakdown in trust. But if expectations are understood from the beginning and revisited when circumstances change, more time will be spent on kingdom impact than in meetings or arguments about unmet expectations. Here are some ways that may help you and your youth pastor gain a clear understanding of each other's expectations.

Be a Coach

Create a coaching relationship with your youth pastor. A coach motivates, inspires, and brings out the best in his team. He doesn't do it through fear; he does it by being at the game, knowing the skills and abilities of each team member, and laying out a game plan that fits the team. Be a coach to your youth pastor by meeting with him regularly, and make sure that some of the time is on his turf.

> Be sure to mention the purpose of your spending time periodically on his turf. If your intentions are not clear, the youth pastor could interpret this to mean you're checking up on him or something's wrong.

Engaging with your youth pastor intentionally once a week will create an environment where you are able to address small issues before they become big problems. You'll also help him gain the confidence to come to you for ministry advice. Meeting on his turf will also give you an opportunity to effectively coach by using teachable moments. Be at the parent meetings your youth pastor runs, and then the next time you meet, you'll be able to speak truth and support from an outside point of view. Go to a youth group night or outreach event.

A coach isn't effective unless he sees the player on the field. If the player just tells him about the performance, the coach can only help him from a very narrow point of view. By watching the game, you will see the team as a whole, and you'll discover how the youth pastor can best lead his team.

> One of the best places to coach a youth pastor is in the area of teaching. We've used a simple feedback process called the 3x3. We've actually whittled it down to 1x1—one thing I did really well. One thing I didn't do so well *and* a suggestion on how to improve it. The key is to remember that you as a senior pastor are *for* your youth leader and vice versa.

As you coach your youth pastor in ministry, there's a potential to mentor him in life as well. If enough trust and respect are established, you may have the opportunity to significantly build into his life. Your investment is then lived out years beyond you.

Create a Handful of "Skill" Expectations

A job description generally covers job responsibility and expectations (even though continued clarity is necessary). Another way to clearly align your expectations with the youth pastor is to have a list of skills that are necessary to be effective in your church. Instead of just answering the question "What do you do?" you'll be answering the equally important question "How do you do your job?" Often it is not the task, but the way in which it was executed that becomes a problem.

> As a senior pastor, be prepared to give some freedom though, to the way in which jobs are performed. We have to give room for our leaders to express their giftedness, even if it's not always the way we would have chosen.

If caring for and communicating with families is one of the skills that a staff member must live out, then it would be pretty clear that 27 unanswered voice mails is unacceptable.

> This could also be associated with a level of professionalism that you expect.

Strategic planning is a skill to help combat procrastination. Staff collaboration as a skill helps "ministry silos" to begin to crumble. Having three to five necessary skills that your staff members (in this case, your youth pastor) must grow in, live out, and use in their job description will define boundaries and empower them to lead.

Having skill expectations also lets your staff know that failure is OK. Too often, staff members don't take risks because they are afraid the end result will be failure. Evaluating them on the way they do their job instead of just on the end result helps to reduce the fear of failure.

Evaluate. Evaluate. Evaluate.

Believe it or not, your youth pastor wants evaluation. He may even crave it. I ask this question of youth pastors at LeaderTreks all the time: "Do you receive personal evaluations from your senior pastor?" Ninety-five percent of the time,

the answer is no. But when I asked them if they would want at least an annual evaluation, it's a resounding *yes!* Evaluation clarifies and confirms your youth pastor's ministry. It encourages him when you acknowledge his job performance and results, and it exposes performance problems that need to be discussed.

> **Especially when evaluation happens proactively and not just reactively. Your youth pastor needs to know that at the end of the day, you have his back. Then he'll be open to all kinds of constructive criticism.**

It also gives him a clear growth strategy to make the necessary changes that will deepen his impact next year.

If you are frustrated or disappointed in your youth pastor or youth ministry, but you've never offered any evaluation, that frustration will only grow deeper and wider, eventually turning to bitterness. And bitterness leaves evidence; even if it's just in body language or listening skills, your youth pastor will pick up on any bitterness or frustration that you hold. The turnover rate for youth pastors is incredibly high, and while that trend occurs for many reasons that don't necessarily pertain to your situation, the process of evaluation can help your youth pastor grow and take confident steps in your church. It will keep him around and help him work through the issues that might hold him back in ministry.

Here are some tips taken from the many surveys of senior pastors on running an effective evaluation:

1. Always make sure your youth pastor knows long before the evaluation what criteria he is being evaluated on: the job description, necessary skills, ability to live out church mission, and so on. Whatever it is, he needs to know ahead of time.

2. Keep evaluations short. Don't go over 45 minutes, or it may become overwhelming for the youth pastor and adjustments will be less likely.

3. Use a scale. Show him where he is with each item (for example, needs work—standard—good—great—excellent).

4. Give three highlights of what he has done well and three action steps for how he can grow in his improvement areas.

5. Next evaluation, make sure to include how he is doing on his action steps.

6. Give him an opportunity to respond and ask questions.

Humility

Where were you in those first years of ministry? Put yourself back there. Were you headstrong and a bit idealistic, or arrogant? Wouldn't you have given your right arm for evaluation, coaching, and help? Remember your early years of ministry, and be gentle with your youth worker—even when it's undeserved or not reciprocated, offer humility.

Whether you are coaching, mentoring, evaluating, or communicating your expectations, *be humble*. While you have a lot to offer your youth pastor, saying it without humility will only be talking at him rather than with him.

Your expectations of your youth pastor need to be clearly communicated and understood for him to effectively execute his job. When your expectations are reasonable and challenging at the same time, and they are clearly communicated, you will set him up for excellence. The following is an evaluation exercise to help you both better understand your expectations of each other.

Expectations

Evaluation

Go through the following three steps, working through how expectations are affecting your relationship with your youth pastor.

If you are going through this book with your youth pastor, take 30 minutes this week to go through this activity together. These three steps coincide with the three steps for him in the youth pastors section.

1. **Job Description**
   Look at your youth pastor's job description. (It might be yellowing from sitting in a file for so long!)

   - On the bottom of the page, write down anything that has been added since it was written (officially added, not just things that have morphed into his routine).

   - Cross out any items that are no longer relevant (such as he used to oversee the children's ministry, but the church has since hired a director for that role.

   - Now go through each item on the page and label it accordingly.

     - F = Fulfilling

     - C = Cannot fulfill (doesn't have the resources or some other factor out of his control)

     - N = Not fulfilling.

   For all the items marked "fulfilling," has he been encouraged or told "job well done"?

   For all the items marked "cannot fulfill," what can you do to equip him or provide the resources he needs to fulfill them?

   For all the items marked "Is not fulfilling," what skills/abilities/disciplines does he need to hone to fulfill these items?

2. **Evaluate**
   If you are going through this exercise with your youth pastor, take 15 minutes to talk through his job description and evaluate what he has done well and areas where he needs improvement. Consider using the format laid out in the chapter. Also, begin talking through some of the skills he needs to hone to be successful at his job in this particular church (also refer back to the chapter). Consider just a handful that you can coach him on and continue to evaluate and provide feedback.

3. **Align Your Expectations**

End this time of evaluation by asking if there's anything you can do to help him. In the youth pastor section of this book, he will have focused on expectations he felt came from the church and which ones were unrealistic versus realistic. Align your expectations by asking what he needs from you. What are some of the unwritten but realistic pressures he is facing, and how can you help coach him through them?

chapter 5

{ senior pastor }

Getting Off the Elevator on the Same Floor...

What a shared mission can do for you

My second youth pastor job was a ton different from my first. When I started, the church threw me a big welcome party, giving me a chance to meet many of the parents and church members. About halfway through the party, a married couple walked up to me and introduced themselves. As I asked questions about them and their family, I soon discovered their immense distaste for the youth group. They told me how their oldest daughter had been introduced to cigarettes at the youth group by other students and was now struggling with the addiction. Because of this they would never allow their youngest daughter to come once she was old enough. It was a hard conversation, and I walked away from the party confused, wondering what I had gotten myself into.

The first few weeks at youth group went really well, except that many of the students continually asked when the smoke break was going to be. I came to learn that the previous youth pastor had let them smoke, would give them regular smoke breaks, and would even stop the church bus on events to let everyone light up on the side of the road. I was really uncomfortable with this and voiced my concerns to the senior pastor. I explained to him my plans to abolish the smoking club our youth group had become, and he backed me completely. He was also really uncomfortable with the situation and just like me, wanted to see the group transformed. In fact, his own daughter had also gotten addicted to smoking, and he too was frustrated. We came up with a plan together of how to move forward.

However, when I announced my plans at the next parent meeting, they were less than enthusiastic. In fact, they were livid. It wasn't because they loved letting their children smoke, but because they were worried their kids would stop coming to youth group. Many of the parents took their concerns to the senior pastor, but to their surprise, he totally backed me. He explained to them how we had come to this decision together and that he was completely supporting me. Even after a bunch of the students left the group, including the senior pastor's own daughter, he still stood by me, encouraging me the whole way. Eventually many of the students came back, without their cigarettes, and even brought their friends. It could never have happened without my senior pastor backing me though. It was an amazing example of us sharing the mission together.

Getting every ministry venture, every age group, and every area to walk in step with one another and toward the same mission requires a lot of work. Take a minute to picture that—every one of your staff members unified, working together, pooling resources, and sharing sacrifices. The kingdom impact of unified leadership in your church would be huge. The Apostle Paul knew the great things awaiting the church if unification happened, but he also understood the difficulties. This dichotomy inspired him to write the church of Ephesus with this charge:

Therefore I, a prisoner for serving the Lord, beg you to lead a life worthy of your calling, for you have been called by God. Always be humble and gentle. Be patient with each other, making allowance for each other's faults because of your love. Make every effort to keep yourselves united in the Spirit, binding yourselves together with peace. For there is one body and one Spirit, just as you have been called to one glorious hope for the future. There is one Lord, one faith, one baptism, and one God and Father, who is over all and in all and living through all (Ephesians 4:1-6).

Amazing outcomes await churches that are unified. Too often it's easy for division to distract us from our mission. You want to know why the teens aren't involved in Sunday morning services, while your youth pastor wants to know why he can't get any adult volunteers for the youth ministry. You want to know why the teens don't participate in the church's service opportunities, while your youth pastor doesn't understand why youth ministry service events don't count as the church's service events.

Your church's mission is like a ship that keeps the entire congregation heading toward the same destination. Division occurs when we begin sending our dinghies and yachts out on excursions. Each boat, carrying a small amount of people, begins exploring the waters in different directions and to different destinations. These new directions may drive us toward different values, different results, and little to no accountability, always ending in disaster. Remember though, that heading to a different destination is different from custom tailoring a ministry. Custom tailoring a ministry still happens on the same ship. The youth ministry (just like the children's ministry and other ministries) meets in a different room, uses different tools, and has a different culture to battle (and leverage) in order to develop teenagers into disciples of Christ. Same goal, different tactics. Same ship, different room.

The great divide happens for many reasons, but it usually happens when both parties begin to make small decisions or shortcuts, leaving room for division. Here are some measures you can take to keep the church unified and on mission.

Get Back to the Who

At the end of the day, you and your youth pastor both serve families (taking into account, of course, that you both serve God first, and serving families is an outflow of that). It's easy to compartmentalize church ministries by age or affiliation, but when a family leaves church, it goes back to the same home. Children, teenagers, and parents are all in this together. If your youth pastor is running an effective ministry and really creating teenagers who own their faith, it will only help that

family. Likewise, if you are able to equip parents to develop disciples of Christ in their children and edify each other in their marriages, it will only help that family. Success in each area of ministry only helps and builds a strong platform for every other ministry. It's easy to get lost in the nitty-gritty of procedures and methodology. And while those things have value, they only have value in the big scope of your mission. Focus on the people you and your youth pastor serve. If you are both effectively serving families, you are headed toward the same ministry destination.

Provide Resources for Growing a Ministry

In addition to financially supporting your youth ministry, think about the physical space you are providing. Does your youth pastor have an adequate and functional place to run a youth ministry? Is he hampered by committee meetings in the next room constantly telling the teenagers to be quiet? Do the students have a space that's conducive to building community and intentional relationships?

Also, build a support system within the church for your youth pastor. Have you advocated the importance of the youth ministry to the entire church? Standing at the pulpit and stating your support and value for the youth ministry will help your youth pastor in untold ways. It will demonstrate the value of volunteering in the youth ministry. It will also create buy-in for the ministry decisions that aren't always supported right away but are the best for the youth. It offers significance to a job that many people unjustly view as just hanging out with kids and playing games.

Lastly, personal growth opportunities for your youth pastor are priceless. Whether it's a mentor inside the church willing to build into him, a budget for books, or time off to meet with the local youth pastor committee, provide resources to help your youth pastor be equipped to grow.

Give Authority to Your Youth Pastor

Youth pastor Greg was getting worn thin by the complaints and demands of parents who wanted him to "fix" their kids. Whether it was behavioral, a struggle in school, or spiritual development, they believed that Greg could (and should) fix it.

Parents made demands about the kind of events that Greg should plan based on their sons' or daughters' interests: a gaming night for the gamers, a worship circle for the musically inclined, a sports ministry for the jocks, and, of course, personal one-on-one mentoring by Greg. He was bombarded with calls from parents disappointed in their kids and complaints that Greg didn't care enough or spend enough time with them.

At his wits' end, Greg and his senior pastor, John, came to a simple conclusion. Parents *are* the primary faith influencers—something Greg had tried to communicate to parents for a while. That is their role. The church was there to uphold and support the families, equipping parents with tools that let them live out their role effectively and help students own their faith. But neither Greg nor anyone else was supposed to fulfill the parents' role.

John and Greg held a parent meeting at the beginning of the school year announcing that the parents, and only the parents, were the primary faith influencers. The more they could accept their role, the more effective the church could be in equipping and supporting families. There was even a set of parent trainings and small groups available to help them, but the role was theirs alone and would not be filled by Greg, John, or anyone else in the church.

That day a huge weight was lifted off Greg's shoulders. He was able to do the ministry he came to the church to do because the senior pastor backed and protected his ability to do that. Greg and John also became incredibly unified that day, bonded together by a common mission.

Use your influence to give authority to your youth pastor. Establish him as a leader you believe in and trust.

> Too often we lead out of fear—fear that our leaders can't and won't lead well, so we see the need to take over. We must stop leading out of fear and must trust instead. We must empower our youth pastors, and we must be supportive when failure happens.

Support in the Midst of Conflict

There's a common story of hurt among youth pastors, shared on countless occasions with me. A disgruntled parent walks into your office with a complaint or an accusation about your youth pastor. You are faced with a tough decision. The person could be right or could be overreacting. But they haven't talked with the youth pastor about it—just you (and possibly other church members).

In order to help your youth pastor succeed—not in winning this battle, but in working in ministry—back him as much as possible. Show the disgruntled member that you are willing to listen but that your youth pastor is a viable member of your team and a leader in the church. Let the member know this offense should be

looked at from the broader scope of the youth pastor's performance and heart and that you choose to believe the best about his heart. Also encourage the member to go directly to the youth pastor and confront the problem rather than only complaining to you.

Go to your youth pastor for information and coaching. Be honest with him. Gather information to see both sides of the story, and then coach him in working through the issue. It may be that the youth pastor messed up and needs coaching to change a behavioral pattern such as using borderline language with students. In that case help him make the change, and then provide an opportunity for reconciliation with the member who came to you. It may be that the member was overreacting and thinks that the students shouldn't play games when they meet on Wednesday night; the youth pastor should extend the Bible study for the whole two hours. In that case, coach your youth pastor in dealing with missed expectations in the church. Help him grow his people skills.

Make sure your youth pastor recognizes and feels like you support him. Even in times of correction, make sure he knows that you believe in him and that you see the situation from a larger perspective. If he feels like you're making a snap judgment or conclusion based on one conversation or gossip about him, it will likely create distance in your relationship with him.

Be Considerate When Making Fundamental Changes

The senior pastor at a large church just finished a great book in the middle of the ministry year on strategic planning and ministries that are built to last. Being inspired and convicted about his church's current method of doing things, he called a staff meeting where he announced that in one month, the entire church would start focusing on the same biblical principles all at the same time. From the nursery to the seniors, everyone would be on the same page. If Sunday preaching focused on Joshua, then every ministry, even small groups, would focus on Joshua as well. If the preaching focused on service, the entire church would focus on service, and even end the series with a churchwide service project.

> We must also be OK when our youth pastor wants to make fundamental changes. We can't simply continue to do ministry the way it has always been done, because no growth will come from it.

While this strategy has proven effective in many churches, the implementation of it in this church divided the staff. What the senior pastor didn't take into

consideration was the number of strategic plans, budgets, hires, and calendars he was affecting. Curriculum had already been bought, service projects had already been planned, and promises had already been made. That semester, the youth group had to cancel three major events—the activities had been promoted, permission slips had been signed, and deposits had been made. Winter camp—one of the churches most intentional and spiritually transformational youth group events—was canceled, because it was the only day that worked for a churchwide service project.

Each ministry worked vigorously to implement this new plan. The cost was huge. But it was such a "good" idea that the senior pastor didn't think through all of the implications of making this change. The grumblings of the staff grew the great divide: "Why couldn't he have waited until the new ministry year?" and "Why weren't we ever asked before we had to turn our departments upside down?"

Many senior pastors use books to grow themselves and develop their leadership. As the books challenge their skills, they look to implement what they've learned into the entire church. A book on evangelism launches a whole new process for the church to adopt and integrate into their ministry (not knowing that the sports ministry is actually incredibly effective at evangelism). A book on spiritual formation launches a new discipleship program (but the high school small group leaders have just finished their training and are now finally running healthy small groups).

Change needs to be implemented, and you are most often the leader of these changes. But the perception of change is usually going to be negative before it's positive. In order to prevent it from dividing your church, especially your youth ministry from the church, spend a lot of time building consensus and buy-in first. As one senior pastor said: "I need to change about 30 things in my church right away. So I've thrown out 29 of them because realistically I can only tackle one of them a year effectively."

Building a shared mission is exhausting. But it's worth it. Each of the action steps in this chapter—and in many cases, in this entire book—are not requirements, but suggestions that can help build a unity that weathers many storms. Ultimately, you know what changes to make and what habits to keep that will best guide your congregation on mission.

Consider these words of encouragement as you lead this week:

And now, a word to you who are elders in the churches. I, too, am an elder and a witness to the sufferings of Christ. And I, too, will share in his glory when he is revealed to the whole world. As a fellow elder, I appeal to you: Care for the flock that God has entrusted to you. Watch over it willingly, not grudgingly—not for what you will get out of it, but because you are eager to serve God (1 Peter 5:1-2).

Here are some exercises for you and your youth pastor to process together that may help you more effectively live in unity together.

Church Family Profile

Assessment

If you are going through this book with your youth pastor, take 30 minutes this week to go through this activity on your own, and then meet with your youth pastor to discuss your thoughts. This assessment coincides with the youth pastor section of the book.

In this activity you will take some time to think about the families in your church. Make sure to go through this activity together with your youth pastor so you can discuss your opinions and reasons behind your thoughts and conclusions.

The goals for this exercise are as follows:

- Describe your view of the families in your church. Explore families' basic needs and areas that could use more attention by combining your observations with your youth pastor's.

- Design a plan for both you and your youth pastor to effectively develop families in your church. The plan should include steps to equip and encourage parents to become teens' primary faith influencers; build marriages that edify both spouses; and help both the parents and their teenagers to develop an owned faith.

Follow these steps to complete the Church Family Profile Assessment:

1. Assign percentages (rough estimates) to each of the items in the Church Family Profile on page 62. Work to come to a consensus on these, using information gleaned from your experiences.

2. If there are percentages you disagree on, discuss why you disagree and listen carefully to each others experiences and involvement with families. It may be that several marriages are in crisis, but all the youth pastor is hearing from his students is that their parents just don't understand them. Several families might be putting on a good front, but the youth pastor has learned some of the behind-the-scenes problems from listening to their kids.

   Take some time to really examine any differences you have in your answers. Also, if any key areas tug at your heart, be sure to discuss them with each other.

3. If there is a demographic issue that is not listed on the Church Family Profile, add that to the chart and assign a percentage to it.

4. Discuss what major issues, patterns, and concerns arise after completing this profile. While both of you are on the same mission of ministering to

families, you may be burdened in different ways, but bringing them to the forefront is important.

5. Lastly, select a few issues or areas of concern that you can team up on to help develop and equip the families in your church based on what you examined in this profile. Create action steps within these areas.

Examples...

- Cast the vision to parents during an event or dessert function describing their role and the church's role in ministering to teenagers.

> Parents = Primary Faith Influencers
>
> Church = Equipping parents to be Primary Faith Influencers, and developing teenagers who will own their faith

- Set up a parenting retreat or a few events that help equip parents of growing teenagers—especially in the areas of greatest need. Partner up as senior pastor and youth pastor to focus on youth culture, a home that cultivates spiritual growth, a Christ-centered family, and other relevant topics.

- Reach out to a specific need area, like single parenting, and spend one training session dealing with specific issues that this brings up.

- Take a month of small groups this year to focus on family dynamics/relationships and a need area from this profile (both for the parents and the youth).

Church Family Profile

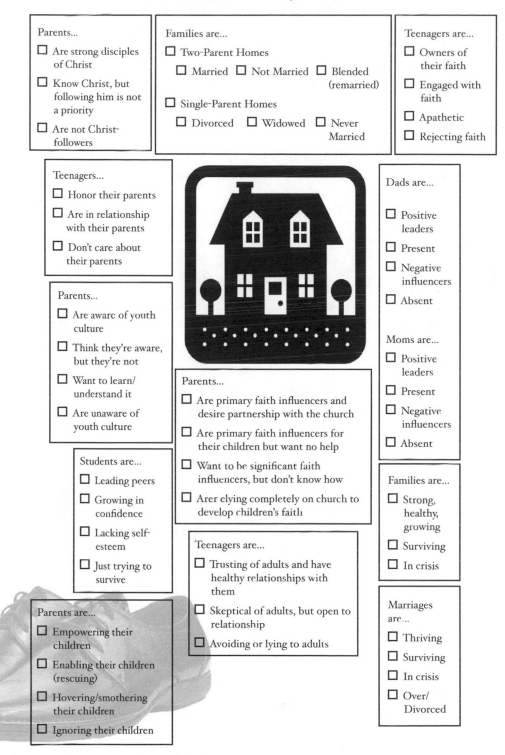

Parents...
- ☐ Are strong disciples of Christ
- ☐ Know Christ, but following him is not a priority
- ☐ Are not Christ-followers

Families are...
- ☐ Two-Parent Homes
  - ☐ Married
  - ☐ Not Married
  - ☐ Blended (remarried)
- ☐ Single-Parent Homes
  - ☐ Divorced
  - ☐ Widowed
  - ☐ Never Married

Teenagers are...
- ☐ Owners of their faith
- ☐ Engaged with faith
- ☐ Apathetic
- ☐ Rejecting faith

Teenagers...
- ☐ Honor their parents
- ☐ Are in relationship with their parents
- ☐ Don't care about their parents

Dads are...
- ☐ Positive leaders
- ☐ Present
- ☐ Negative influencers
- ☐ Absent

Parents...
- ☐ Are aware of youth culture
- ☐ Think they're aware, but they're not
- ☐ Want to learn/ understand it
- ☐ Are unaware of youth culture

Moms are...
- ☐ Positive leaders
- ☐ Present
- ☐ Negative influencers
- ☐ Absent

Parents...
- ☐ Are primary faith influencers and desire partnership with the church
- ☐ Are primary faith influencers for their children but want no help
- ☐ Want to be significant faith influencers, but don't know how
- ☐ Arer elying completely on church to develop children's faith

Students are...
- ☐ Leading peers
- ☐ Growing in confidence
- ☐ Lacking self-esteem
- ☐ Just trying to survive

Families are...
- ☐ Strong, healthy, growing
- ☐ Surviving
- ☐ In crisis

Teenagers are...
- ☐ Trusting of adults and have healthy relationships with them
- ☐ Skeptical of adults, but open to relationship
- ☐ Avoiding or lying to adults

Parents are...
- ☐ Empowering their children
- ☐ Enabling their children (rescuing)
- ☐ Hovering/smothering their children
- ☐ Ignoring their children

Marriages are...
- ☐ Thriving
- ☐ Surviving
- ☐ In crisis
- ☐ Over/ Divorced

conclusion

{ senior pastor }

Throughout the process of writing this book, I've loved talking with youth pastors and senior pastors from around the country, and remembering my days as a youth pastor. But at the same time, a lot of sadness has come as I've hashed over old stories from my days in the church. Sadness, not because of what happened, but because of what didn't happen. Looking back, I realize now I did not truly see my relationship with any of my senior pastors the way I should have seen it. I never put the time and effort into building that relationship and now, years down the road, I realize I am disconnected from the people I partnered alongside in ministry. Where I should have lasting friendships, I have nothing.

But it does not have to be this way. When you and your youth pastor are connected, you can truly serve and meet the needs of your congregation. Being united with your youth pastor helps you build momentum and excitement for the church staff and elder team. The kingdom difference is far greater as your impact now spreads to the youth ministry and your youth pastor's impact spreads to adults. Obstacles and challenges are all minimized. The future of your church becomes a place of excitement and dreaming, instead of a place of surviving and quitting. And at the end of the day, you'll be doing ministry—and life—with a trusted friend.